AF324006

Responsible Global Governance

The Authors :

RITA DULCI RAHMAN has 26 years of experience in international relations
in different fields, among others in trade and investment, migration, conflict
resolution, and development co-operation. She has been committee member
or chair in several European and Dutch governmental and non governmental
bodies such as EECOD, CCME, ECLOF and Fondad. Born in the Dutch
Antilles, she is currently Minister Plenipotentiary at the Royal Netherlands
Embassy in New Delhi. She obtained her Masters degree in Development
Studies at the University of Leiden, Netherlands, and her Bachelors in Mathematics, University of Surinam. For three years (1988-1991) she taught at
the University of Leiden. She has published more than 30 articles on international relations.

JOSE MIGUEL ANDREU is Professor of Economics at the University of
Sevilla, Spain. He has also taught Economics in the Basque Country University, in the University of Alcala de Henares, and in the Open University of
Spain (UNED). For 30 years he has been delivering lectures on Introduction
to Economics, Intermediate Macroeconomics, Superior Macroeconomics,
Theory of Economic Growth, Money and Banking etc. He has published
several textbooks for students, reports, and more than a hundred articles on
Spanish and international economic matters. For two years (1981-1982) he
was economic advisor to the Prime Minister of Spain. Recently (2000-2003)
he served as a Spanish diplomat to India.

Responsible Global Governance

A Programme for World Stability and Institutional Reform

Rita Dulci Rahman
Jose Miguel Andreu

Academic Foundation NEW DELHI
www.academicfoundation.com

First Published in 2004 by
ACADEMIC FOUNDATION
4772-73 / 23 Bharat Ram Road,
(23 Ansari Road), Darya Ganj,
New Delhi - 110 002. INDIA.

Phones : 23245001, 02, 03, 04.
Fax : +91-11-23245005.
e-mail : academic@vsnl.com
www : academicfoundation.com

Responsible Global Governance :
A Programme for World Stability and Institutional Reform
by Rita Dulci Rahman and Jose Miguel Andreu
ISBN 81-7188-352-4

Designed and typeset by Italics India, New Delhi
and printed at Print Perfect, New Delhi.

For those who dare putting people first.

Contents

1

Introduction

Few people could imagine after the crumbling of the Soviet Union at the beginning of the 90s, that the issue of national security would again gather momentum only a decade later. Indeed, the resulting change in the world power structure of those days seemed to point out that the assumed new hegemonic power[1], the US, could easily act as the sole leader and arbiter in all economic and political matters. This new hegemonic power of the US was mainly based on its enormous military expenditure and on its dominance in international economic institutions.

In the 90s the US leadership under the Clinton administration seldom acted without seeking support or at least concurrence of the UN, EU and others. But at the same time his administration, with its supremacy, remained selective in its commitments and did not apply the same criteria to similar problems in the world, as one could have expected from a superpower with lasting moral authority. These selective operations occurred not only in political issues, many a time a matter of opinion, but also in some areas of consent, such as environment.

Along these at times uncomfortable political facts of the 90s, a new era of extreme optimism seemed to appear on the economic horizon, a mix of indefinite and assumed world wide economic growth stemming from the outcome of a purported new theory, baptised as "new economics". A theory that, although rejecting the very existence of the business cycle, succumbed soon after its birth, to the first downturn that appeared at the end of the 90s.

---

1. As recently proven in the aftermath of the war in Iraq, although the US has an enormous high-tech weaponry, the human factor of its army is clearly insufficient and over stretched for the purported role of policemen in the world without the co-operation of the rest of the international community.

Unfortunately for the mirage believers of the 90s, neither the economic nor the political cycles had passed away. Indeed, months before the terrorist attack on the twin towers in New York, and just weeks after the neo-conservative[2] Bush administration came into power, the economic bubble that had started as a consequence of the tremendous wave of optimism in Western countries, burst and the expected indefinite growth vanished. Reckless over-investments mainly in the IT sector, based on massive attraction to stock markets of greedy but naïve savers, lured by a breed of new specialists in financial engineering, some of them no more than ordinary crooks, played a major role in the economic downturn.

The fantasists of the 90s, and behind them governments, mainly focusing on the exceptional growth rate of productivity in the US in the second half of the decade, conveniently neglected economic disaster elsewhere. The hasty liberalisation and privatisation at all costs in the former Soviet Union, based on imposed Washington Consensus policies[3] (IMF, World Bank, US Treasury), became a straightaway nightmare for its citizens. Following the recommended economic reform policies, Russia experienced an economic disaster.

In the booming 90s, little to no attention was given to cumulative violent outbursts of longstanding conflicts in the periphery of the North, say in the Middle East, Africa, South Asia and even within the borders of Europe[4]. The assumed irrelevance of these conflicts was a clear mistake given the fact that these

---

2. The economic and political actions of the Bush administration at international scale have been labelled as "neo-conservative" to distinguish them from traditional conservative policies of the Republicans. The most outstanding difference between these two approaches is the disputable new policy of unilateral pre-emptive strikes, adopted by the neo-conservative leadership. Mailer, N (2003: 60). Why are we at war? A Random House Paperback New York.

3. What John Williamson, of the Institute for International Economics in Washington, DC, has called the Washington Consensus describes the conditions considered as necessary for a poor country to get itself on a path of sustained development. These necessary conditions to be fulfilled, also known as "the only right policy" is shared by a number of Washington based leading international economic institutions (World Bank and IMF) and by the US Treasury. The main conditions of this Consensus are: no inflation; sound fiscal policies; broader tax bases and more moderate marginal rates; free internal markets and liberalisation of the external ones including the exchange rate; export orientation of the economies; public expenditure more tilted to investment in infrastructure; health and education, and to the fight against poverty.

4. A list of "forgotten disasters" and "forgotten crisis" was recently published in "The Economist". Nov. 22. 2003, pg.46.

conflicts were not only rooted in tribalism, traditional religious or ethnic tensions as presumed, but mainly in economic backwardness. A recent study on 52 civil wars since 1960 in the world, has clarified that, contrary to conventional wisdom, ethnic tensions and ancient political feuds are rarely the primary cause of civil war. Instead economic forces such as entrenched poverty and heavy dependence on exports of natural resources are usually to blame[5]. Clearly the global community should have made a far greater effort to prevent escalation of the existing poverty gap into violent conflicts. It was and it is unacceptable to remain inactive at cost of tremendous human suffering when the means to prevent it are at hand.

We agree with Nobel Prize winner Joseph Stiglitz[6] on the idea that the way in which globalisation[7] has been managed, including the international trade agreements and reform policies based on Washington Consensus, need to be rethought radically. September 11 has confronted the entire global community with the fact that we share a single planet and that human security[8] of its citizens should concern us all. We will have to follow rules to live together, rules that must be, and must be seen, as fair and just for powerful and poor alike, in all corners of the world. These rules for world stability and (human) security, as well as their working, will have to strongly reflect a basic sense of respect, mutual responsibility and social justice.

1.1. Poverty and access to full information

Despite repeated promises on poverty reduction which were made through the whole booming period of the 90s, the number of people living on less than \$2 a day has actually increased by almost 100

---

5. World Bank Press Review 16 May 2003.

6. Stiglitz, J. (2002: Preface) Globalisation and its Discontents. Penguin Books India, 2003.

7. Globalisation could be defined as the removal of barriers to trade and movements of factors, in order to reach a closer integration of national economies.

8. (Human) Security is no longer only the protection of territorial integrity and political sovereignty. It also includes the protection of societies and citizens from physical violence, and from poverty, deprivation, discrimination and environmental degradation. Rahman, R.D. and Andreu, J.M. (2002a: 11) Financing Economic Development and Human Security. Rashtriya Printers, New Delhi.

million[9]. And this has occurred with ongoing problems in access to safe drinking water, food, employment, shelter and treatment of poverty related diseases. Note also that almost 2 billion people live in countries that are neither globalising nor developing. In these countries the per capita GDP has experienced stagnation or even reductions along the 90s.

These problems of poverty and ignorance, for long considered mainly as national and isolated issues inside LDC[10] and developing countries, in the late 80s and 90s progressively changed into a global matter with doubtless negative spill-over effects[11] on the rich world. Far from recognising this mutation and trying to understand its causes, which perhaps would have triggered financial efforts and imaginative solutions, the leadership of Western countries remained insensitive. The most outstanding examples of this lack of long-term acumen of Western governments have been the fast decrease in the ongoing insufficient, bilateral development aid on the one hand, and on the other the rather inefficient and short-term approaches of rich countries in international economic negotiations.

In addition, the information revolution of the late 80s and 90s acted as a catalyst for rising new and legitimate expectations among the poor in developing countries. Suddenly the poor, even in remote villages, became aware of the fact that they had been, and still are, bad treated or neglected by the West. This awareness was engendered by broad access to a full, life, and cheap information over global developments, over-consumption in the rich world and unfair distribution of wealth.

This new consciousness seems to us a replication of the one that appeared in current rich countries at the dawn of the 20th century,

---

9. World Development Report 2000. World Bank, Washington DC. Note however that if we use the definition of poverty as the number of people with income under 1$ a day (the so-called poverty line), the volume of poverty has in recent years mildly decreased.

10. The acronym LDC refers to the so-called 44 "Least Developed Countries" according to terminology of the World Bank. In this essay these LDC are often included in the general expression "developing countries".

11. Revolution in transports (cost, speed and accessibility), growing awareness in LDC of the economic gap that traps them, and easy access to full information on living conditions elsewhere, have strongly increased push and pull migration factors in LDC and the development of underground economic activities. As a consequence, bogus asylum seekers, illegal migration, trafficking in human beings, drugs trafficking and other forms of smuggling, boomed.

which provoked internal political and economic turmoil, conducive to a period of instability in Europe, ultimately escalating into two dramatic world wars. Perhaps this instability and wars could have been prevented with an earlier introduction of the welfare state, as a lubricant in the often-difficult relations between the economic agents. Hence our call for a rational effort to urgently bridge the poverty and exclusion gap between rich and poor countries, in order to avoid a further fall in human security and to reach global stability, be it in Bali, Istanbul or New York.

1.2. The appearance of a new type of insecurity

Before the collapse of the Soviet Union, the international political situation based on two opposing ideologies generated a sense of security, which was different from the current one. Up to the 90s, the countries of NATO and Warsaw-Pact appeared to be in equilibrium based on a relentless arms race and dissemination of inaccurate information. Nevertheless the mutual threat during the cold war created some feelings of insecurity in the two blocs, although somewhat ambiguous. In this period in many developing countries the sentiment of insecurity was experienced differently, in particular in those countries in which the two blocs were in direct armed confrontation.

In the 90s the appearance of a hegemonic power, and the disappearance of the communist alternative, has changed the security feelings in different ways. First of all the perception of insecurity has increased in many developing countries, in particular in those countries no longer interesting for the rich world because they lacked relevant resources, while their geopolitical meaning has faded away. These are countries mainly in Africa and Central America.

However, also in the West a new feeling of insecurity emerged in a generalised way: the fear for international terrorism. Consequently one cannot deduce that 12 years after the crumbling of the Soviet Union, the world is more secure than before or at least significantly secure. This means that the policies deployed by Western leadership at a world scale to enhance security, be this political or economic, have not worked properly in the past decade.

Note that up to the 90s, while in some developing countries the bloody battle of the East-West conflict took place, many other poor countries enjoyed security by being in alliance with the leadership of one of the two blocs. To be consistent they also aligned their economic policies with the corollaries of one of the two models[12] considered as optima, while internal social pressure in these countries was shrewdly cushioned, blaming the other bloc for internal economic failures. Often the leadership of either bloc (US or USSR) competed in influence for gaining political alliance by means of both arms and financial support. Finally, a meaningful number of so-called "non-aligned" countries opted for a "third way", and remained flirting with leaders of both blocs.

Hence, before the crumbling of the Soviet Union most developing countries and LDC were somehow part of the international power structure since they either belonged to one of the two blocs or to the Non-aligned movement. The power shift in the 90s also influenced the economic prospects of many developing countries. This has been clearly visible in international trade negotiations and public aid transfers, wherein rich countries imposed asymmetric criteria and conditions. Often this was done with an attitude of "take it or leave it", apparently because "beggars cannot be choosers". No wonder that, in many developing countries frustrations have reached untenable levels[13].

As a consequence, the hope of many poor countries has become bleak, since their own security and prosperity concerns are no longer

---

12. For more than one century, two economic models for understanding economic behaviour remained in competition. On the one hand, the Marxist model, which explained the working of the economy, based on the theory of the value of labour. This was a theory that, having been useful to explain some economic phenomena by classical economists (Smith and Ricardo), was mainly abandoned with the arrival of the Marginalist School in the last third of the 19th century. While in the following decades the Marginalist School, also called neo-classicism, made enormous advances in understanding microeconomic behaviour of firms and consumers, and capitalists and workers, the alternative school of Marxists did not produce significant improvements in the explanation of the economic phenomena and remained attached to its internal dogma (labour-value theory, exploitation and surplus). As it is now well acknowledged, with the contributions of Joan Robinson and others, the concepts of exploitation, monopolistic profits and unequal interchange can be explained inside the neo-classical model. No wonder that despite the isolated and sterile efforts to update the Marxist model, carried out by Sraffa (1960), this model ended in historical files.

13. Despite this, in the 90s the average annual growth rate of exports from low and middle income countries (in terminology of the WB) was significantly higher (9%) than the average of the world (5.8%) or than the average of the high income economies (4.9%). World Bank (2003: 315), "03 World Development Indicators".

on the international agenda, which is dominated by an overdone conception of security and protection of own prosperity in the rich world. This has been conducive to exaggerated controls on people and commodities coming from the South.

Without having to consider any countervailing power[14], the current US administration in its war against international terrorism, has at times abandoned multilateralism, imposing its will by armed interventions.

The main argument used by the current US leadership to justify its new interventionist strategy is that national security forces them to unleash pre-emptive attacks against states hosting or equipping terrorists[15]. This new unilateral interventionist policy of the US has not only significantly undermined multilateral institutions, but also its own image. First by entangling in overt logrolling activities in the Security Council, and second by means of averting resolutions when logrolling fails.

However the reality has proved that after two US lead interventions in poor countries, the creation of political stability and reconstruction has so far not been reached and prospects for the future are uncertain. Consequently the threat of pre-emptive military intervention by the hegemonic power, even to force regime change, has paradoxically become a real concern for global development and human security in our days.

Summing up, instead of greater stability, the end of cold war has progressively generated new types of instability and insecurity[16]. But curiously, the longing for security has also re-linked poor and rich communities in a new and unexpected way.

---

14. The existence of countervailing powers is a fundamental premise of democracy, be this national or international. In economics the absence of countervailing powers is conducive to abusive monopolies and in politics to authoritarian behaviour. Any *ad hoc* argument against this principle is pure demagogy.

15. For a consideration on the historical background of pre-emptive actions, vide "The Economist" (2003: 25) Nov. 22nd. "Binding the colossus".

16. Human security as the contra-pole of human insecurity is the freedom from fear, the freedom from hunger and the freedom from want, as explained by Truman, the US President at the inauguration of the UN in 1948. September 11 has altered this definition by adding the need to secure citizens from terrorist attacks.

1.3. September 11 and disputes on its causes

It is generally recognised that the so-called globalisation has only brought benefits to a limited number of countries[17], and inside them to some individuals[18]. In effect, far from improving the distribution of income at a global scale, globalisation has generated a worse distribution and an increased gap, while the interest of the rich in bridging the gap and in understanding the poverty cause seems to have faded away.

Against this background, 11 September 2001 occurred. Although this action of international terrorism was appalling and has rightly been condemned by almost everyone, the decades-long inaction of rich countries against poverty and political exclusion of many communities should also be cast off. Suddenly, the shocking act carried out by a terrorist organisation changed the minds of many leaders in the world. The up to then optimistic economists and politicians changed their views overnight and drastically.

The changes however, went in two directions. The main affected side, the US, declared an international war at all costs against a somewhat invisible enemy, irrespective of whether this war could be gained in a couple of months or in the long term. Although the two battles fought so far in this international war have gathered some international support, they have also generated large scale criticism. First, because of hasty implementation, not emptying intelligence and diplomatic mediation, second because of military overkill, third because of the lack of post-war planning for stability and reconstruction, and fourth because of the inability to reach the initial proclaimed targets.

---

17. Maddison, A (2001: 129) "The World Economy. A Millennium Perspective. OECD, Paris. In this publication it is explained that 168 countries (40 countries of Asia, 44 countries of Latin America, 27 countries of Eastern Europe, and 57 countries of Africa) have experienced in the so-called neo-liberal period (1973-1998) an average annual growth rate of their per capita GDP of minus 0.21%. Note that the 57 countries of Africa have experienced no growth at all in their per capita GDP in this period, while the per capita GDP of the Eastern Europe countries had slumped to an annual rate of minus 1.1% Even more the per capita GDP of the slow-growth 40 selected countries of Asia experienced in this neo-liberal period an average growth rate (0.59%) almost similar (0.48%) to that reached in colonial times (1870-1913).

18. It is clear that "not everyone in the United States share in general prosperity (...). America's economic progress left at least 20 or 30 million people at the bottom of the distribution, slipping backward". Krugman, P. (2000: 19). The return of depression economics. Penguin Books.

Other politicians and world leaders, somewhat more at a distance and perhaps with more acumen, started a call for bridging the economic and political gap as a precondition to curb further spread of terrorism in the world. Speaking to the International Herald Tribune after September 11, President James Wolfensohn of the World Bank[19] remarked: " We know that exclusion can breed violent conflict... in which poverty is a central ingredient. It is time for many to reflect on how to make the world a better and safer place, ...addressing poverty is addressing peace." In a similar way, Gordon Brown, British Chancellor of the Exchequer, stressed the importance of increasing official development aid (ODA), which in real terms had been in frank decline in the 90s, and suggested the implementation of a "new Marshall Plan" financed by all rich countries. On the occasion he, referring to the new global interrelations among societies, stated that "what happened to poorest citizens in poor countries can affect the richest in the richest ones".

1.4. Irrational reactions

Against this background, the scheduled UN meeting to increase development aid to poor countries held in Monterrey in March 2002, was in many aspects a good opportunity and a timely event for rich countries to take effective measures against the growing gap. As recently explained[20], those measures, if taken, could complement, and in midterm substitute, further military actions against international terrorism. However, the Monterrey meeting became a failure mainly because of the shortsightedness of some Western countries, which, after dislodging the former regime of Afghanistan, considered this military action as a sufficient model for the solution of the problem.

In fact, just a few months after September 11, no serious attempt was made by the donor community to look into possibilities for an effective fight against poverty at a global scale. No special attention was paid to alarming disparities of per capita GDP in already conflictive countries. Instead of that they limited themselves in Monterrey to supply a simplistic recipe, which in quantitative terms

---

19. International Herald Tribune, October 27, 2001.
20. Rahman, RD. and Andreu, JM. (2002a: 82), book already mentioned.

was not even in line with the UN and World Bank proposals. They rejected the UN proposal of increasing ODA up to 0.5% of the donors GDP, from the current rate of 0.23 %, while the old UN aid target of 0.7%, committed in 1970, was not even mentioned.

Surprisingly, and against lessons learned from hasty liberalisation and sub-optimal sequencing of policies in recent economic history, donor countries in Monterrey stressed the convenience of a larger financial involvement of the private sector and multinational corporations (MNC) in the fight against poverty in LDC. Instead of significantly increasing and reorganising their development aid (public funding), the donor countries proposed a meagre increase in official involvement and more restrictive conditions for access to these funds.

As expressed by the donors, the development approach applied in the 90s to support developing countries had not worked properly. In their view, this approach had not created enough responsibility among the governments of the recipient LDC, thus squandering a significant part of the transferred resources. Note however that this consideration, as Gordon Brown has recently acknowledged[21], openly ignores the problems that confront governments in poor countries for financing primary public goods, such as basic infrastructure, health and education. These primary public goods, indispensable for enhancing private activities, cannot and will not be financed by foreign private-sector (due to lack of sufficient returns at short term for most of the projects). Besides, in the past the private sector did not play this role inside the donor countries either.

Given the fact that there is scant short term substitution capacity between public and private foreign finance in most LDC, and that FDI does not enter significantly in LDC with deficient infrastructures and human resources, a reorganised external public funding should change into the main source for financing these primary public goods. Consequently, as we will explain, international public financing by the rich countries should be boosted, pooled and reshuffled, and complemented by larger facilities to poor countries in international trade in order to boost their development.

---

21. Brown, G. (2003). Presentation of a new proposal for financing development in the IMF. Note from an article of Griffiths, B. in "The Economic Times", India. 14.4.2003.

The amount of international public financing to ignite the process should be an issue for further discussion. As mentioned earlier, proposals of Brown, Wolfensohn, and UN (Annan) focused on 0.5% of donors GDP[22]. Although these proposals would double the current scant and relatively declining ODA, we do believe that this figure can by no means solve *in a reasonable period of time* the increasingly pressing social claims in LDC, and thus it cannot help to bring global stability.

Since the IT revolution and the greater accessibility to global information has stepped up the tempo of history, development financing should urgently be increased and reorganised. Against the opinion of some short-sighted leaders, this action would play in favour of all, including the donor communities, while at the same time this process would enhance international social justice and help to achieve international public goods (peace and human security). Observe that this policy would not divert from the neo-classical model, but it would simply be a sustainable approach to it.

1.5. A new approach for conflict resolution: institutional reform

As we have described before, the persistence of unsolved conflicts due to exclusion and poverty, growing economic gap, imposition of Washington Consensus policies and asymmetric negotiations and rules within WTO, complemented by negative feelings over international policies deployed by Western leadership, seems to have generated a new kind of instability and insecurity in the world. On the other hand a working policy to increase global stability and security in the context of the current United Nations, seems unlikely, if not impossible, given the power structure stemming from the ruling charter of the UN.

In our view a significant part of the current instability could be attributed to an ill-implemented globalisation, based on a rather

---

22. Recently, in a comment on the G-8 Summit in Evian, Sachs, J.D. has mentioned that "G-8 leaders should commit to provide adequate financing for the Global Fund to fight AIDS, Tuberculosis and Malaria, to raise productivity in Africa,..., to ensure that all poor children have the opportunity to go to school,..., (and) to ensure that all poor people have access to clean drinking water and sanitation. The total cost of this agenda, remarkably, would be much less than 1% of the annual income of rich countries". Sachs, J.D. (2003) en "Securing the world's future at Evian." Taken from "The Economic Times", 03-06-03, New Delhi.

selfish and short-sighted agenda driven by the West. As a consequence there is a need for democratisation and institutional change of the multilateral institutions, not only of the IMF and the World Bank, but also of the UN system as a whole[23].

First of all, the international financial institutions should be reorganised, as they play a central role in the management of globalisation, while their decision making procedures still coincides with the power play as designed in the outdated charter of the UN. Secondly because the UN necessarily has to correct its capability to enforce its own resolutions, and thirdly because the current UN, with the privileges of some member countries hinders the creation of necessary countervailing powers in a reasonable period of time, in order to gain international political equilibrium.

These institutional changes will improve global stability, since the current political representation structure of the UN is far from the democratic principle of a direct relation between the number of represented people and the effective number of issued votes (in the Security Council, General Assembly, etc). It is also desirable that at shot-term qualified majorities in decision making substitute veto-rights in the Security Council[24].

In our view, to ease the process of democratisation of the UN it would be convenient to count with a homogenous and "united" EU to balance international power sharing. But that will require a significant change of the political organisation of the European Union, which in our view should move towards a federation of countries interested in combining foreign policies as well as security policies along with economic progress[25].

Perhaps many US citizens could consider that the existence of countervailing powers would have a negative impact on their interest.

---

23. Although Stiglitz has rightly emphasised the failures of the Washington Consensus and WTO, we do believe that his suggestions for institutional reform are bound to fail if the main multilateral body, the UN, is not significantly reformed. Vide Stiglitz (2002: 223), book already mentioned.

24. In the past months Kofi Annan has called for an urgent reform of the Security Council. In his words: "Unless the Security Council regains the confidence of the states and world public opinion, individual states will increasingly resort exclusively to their own national perception of emerging threats and how best to deal with them" Vide "The Economist" (2003: 26) Nov. 22nd.

25. Rahman, R.D. and Andreu, J.M. (2002b: 94). A Federation with Enlargement for European Prosperity. Rashtriya Printers, New Delhi.

The reality however is that the current traits of the US governance, with a variable and sometimes unilateral policy[26], devised many times on a case by case basis and founded on its economic and military power, cannot be sustainable in a democratic and informed world. Precisely in a world in which US citizens are less than 5 % of the global population.

1.6. Content of the book

Our global society is undergoing unbalanced developments and is facing serious problems, briefly described in the paragraphs above. Without counterbalance, these developments and problems might move us into further decline in human security and even into social and economic stagnation. At present, events in the most remote areas of our planet can influence the core of affluent societies, while access to information on the effects and on the events themselves is more wide spread than ever.

As the entire world, petrified with fear, could watch the crumbling of the twin towers, ordinary people immediately started expressing their concern and pressing for more human security and for a fundamental change in global governance. But the people in the streets do not make policies. Hence our call for fast multilateral institutional reform and for the pooling and boosting of resources to bridge the poverty gap.

In order to give a solid foundation to our suggestions for the way ahead and to present our programme, Chapter 2 will start a discussion on the basic traits of the current mainstream economics. Analysing the features of mainstream interpretation of the so-called "unique model", its theoretical weaknesses, and its outputs in the 90s will guide us. In Chapter 3, after considering the historical evolution of macro-economic magnitudes of the different blocs or big

---

26. As stated by Harold Hongju Koh, Professor of International Law at Yale, and former Assistant Secretary of State for Human Rights in the Clinton Administration, in a lecture delivered in London on 21 October 2003: "People living outside America sometimes suggest that the reason is rooted in the American national culture of unilateralism, parochialism and an obsession with power. With respect, let me urge you to see it differently. The Bush doctrine, I believe is less a broad manifestation of Americ an national character than of short-sighted decisions made by a particularly extreme American administration". Taken from "The Economist" 2003, 1 November, page 25.

countries, with special reference to the Muslim world and to the US-EU increasing gap, we will look into the behaviour of international economic institutions and international power sharing.

The current economic and political traits are being discussed in Chapter 4. Once the former considerations have been finalised, we devote special attention in Chapter 5 to historical precedents in relation to current growing gaps in the context of well-informed societies. In this Chapter we will also discuss possible political and economic reactions of developing countries, which could occur if their cases remains neglected. Before drawing conclusions we outline in Chapter 6 the necessary international economic and institutional changes to correct the current trends in order to gain security, sustainability and prosperity for all.

2

Recent Evolution of
Economic Philosophy

2.1. Evolution of mixed economies of market

Handbooks of economic theory distinguish three systems to organise economic life. These are pure capitalism, pure socialism and the mixed economy of market. All these systems could be defined as ways of economic organisation through which societies answer the fundamental questions to be solved by the economy: what to produce, how to produce and for whom to produce.

2.1.1. Pure capitalism and mixed economies of market

In simple words we could define a system of pure capitalism as that in which most of the physical assets of production are owned privately, while the bulk of economic decisions are made inside markets by private agents (families or firms). In such a context the economic role played by the public sector will be minimal. Just the creation and maintenance of the strictly necessary domestic public goods: defence, justice, security and some infrastructure. Conversely, a system of pure socialism is one in which most of the physical productive assets are owned or controlled by the public sector, which at the same time makes the bulk of decisions, not only related to production but also to consumption. However, these definitions are ideal. In reality the economic systems have always been a mix of the former two pure systems, with positioning either closer to one or the other extreme, or sometimes in the middle referred to as mixed economies of market.

Mixed economies of market are logically a lukewarm combination of the two pure systems. In this system, the private agents (families or firms) acting for their own interest, determine with their actions what to produce, how to produce and for whom to produce, but this occurs within the framework of a certain degree of government intervention. In these economies agents have to commit themselves to four main principles: 1) the supremacy of private ownership, supported by the rule of law; 2) the freedom of contracting; 3) the existence of competitive markets; and 4) a limited and predictable role, played by the public sector.

2.1.2. *Economic and social failures*

Certainly no economic system can completely adjust to the ideal concept of "laissez fair". This is due to the existence of the so-called "economic or social market failures"[27] that the public sector will have to amend. Particularly in relation to the so-called "public goods"[28] which can only be financed through taxes.

The alleged historical trend towards concentration of certain manufacturing productions in a few private firms brought many governments to introduce anti-monopolistic regulations, which were difficult to administrate. In some cases, in order to promote competence, governments were even encouraged to create public firms in these industries[29]. However, history has proved, that these pro-competitive strategies have been less effective than a strategy of gradually opening these industries to international competition.

Another historical reason for progressive government interventions in the sphere of private activities has had to do with the so-called "externalities". These are phenomena which, being by-products of certain productive or consumptive activities, generate external effects, be these positive (e.g. water harvesting) or negative (e.g. polluting industrial waste, sewage) in the production or

---

27. These market failures, be these economic (tendency to develop monopolies, existence of public goods, appearance of externalities or lack of complete information) or social (considered social unfair results of the free-market system), are conducive to non-optima situations that governments have to correct. Stiglitz, J. (2000: 77) Economics of the public sector. 3rd Ed. Norton.

28. These are goods for collective and not for individual use or consumption, reason why private agents would never pay individually and willingly for its supply, preferring to behave as "free riders". This is why the public sector will have to finance such goods, by establishing taxes. Note that historically the list of public goods (pure or impure, also called club-goods) has become progressively larger.

29. The introduction of public firms to increase competition, while neglecting the option of opening markets, created an additional amount of uncertainty by blurring the border that should separate the field of action of the public and private sectors.

consumption of other agents, or in the environment. The existence of these externalities have induced many governments to establish subsidies or taxes to the consumption or production of certain goods, in order to balance social profits of these activities with their social costs[30]. Additionally, the need to spread "correct information" for a better working of markets has also been an additional reason for growing public intervention.

Letting aside the former sources of growing public intervention based on the economic failures of markets we should not forget other interventions in relation to the "social failures" of these markets. It is a matter of fact that market economies tend to generate quantities and prices that, although being competitive and therefore efficient, could socially be considered inadequate or even unfair[31]. Given the fact that certain individuals or collectives involved in these social failures could be doomed to non-desirable situations, according to the prevalent social ideas about the bearable minimum standard of living, public sectors have intervened in their favour by means of establishing transfer policies. These interventions have been internal ones such as public pension schemes or subsidised education and health, or external ones such as ODA.

Complementary to the transfer policies, "progressive taxes" were introduced along the first three-quarters of the 20th century, for reaching a more egalitarian distribution of income. Precisely the existence of these progressive taxes, in connection with the inflation and the growth phenomena, enabled Western countries to automatically reap larger public revenues, thus making it easier for the public sector to enter into additional activities.

Finally we should not forget some other arguments which up to the 80s induced growing public intervention: the active promotion of economic stability by means of management of aggregate demand,

---

30. In certain cases, when property rights are well defined and the number of parties involved is limited, it is possible to obtain the same results letting the (private) parties negotiate among themselves. Coase, W. (1960) "The Problem of Social Cost", Journal of Law and Economics, October.

31. Certain individuals (or collectives) that start their lives (development process) with scant capital resources because of limited inheritance, or scant human resources because of lack of capacity due to malnutrition, health deficiencies, or low level of education, could be incapable of obtaining decent incomes or even could not obtain any income.

and active policies to encourage economic growth. These two modern-times targets pursued by public authorities were expected to promote full employment and to curb inflation. In order to achieve these targets, governments developed fiscal, expenditure and monetary policies along with other initiatives.

2.2. Discussion on the size of the public sector

The share of the public sector in the western economies grew during the major part of the 20th century[32], in particular between the Second World War and the late 70s. At the end of the 70s a general feeling that the public sector in Western countries, more in particular in Europe, were oversized and often inefficient, gained strong political support.

Although few economists would reject the belief that public sectors have a number of unquestionable functions, including that of income distribution not stemmed from the markets, in the 70s the issue of the size of the public sector and some of its functions came under scrutiny.

The theory of Public Choice[33], the basic assumption of which is that all the agents in the field of politics (voters, politicians and bureaucrats) act mainly in their own interest, highlighted the possibility that the public sector activities, as those of the private ones, could be submitted to "failures". According to this theory, similar to the way in which consumers and private firms try to maximise their satisfaction or profits, politicians and bureaucrats play with the core target of maintaining their jobs and supporting their

---

32. Maddison, A. (1989: 71). "The World Economy in the Twentieth Century". OECD. Note that in some western countries, the public sector has grown even after the 70s.

33. The theory of Public Choice was developed by different economists, such as the Nobel-awarded James Buchanan, Gordon Tulloch and others. Previously, in 1942, Jozef Schumpeter pioneered the theory of the Public Choice in some parts of his famous publication titled "Capitalism, Socialism and Democracy". Kenneth Arrow, another Nobel-prize winner, studied mathematically the difficulties to establish collective priorities in consistency with individual values, in his publication "Social Choice and Individual Values" (1951). Anthony Downs, already in 1957, explained in his work "Economic Theory of Democracy" that the main target of politicians when proposing economic policies is to be re-elected, something that happens in every democracy, regardless of whether it relates to a developed or a developing country.

own careers. As such the general interests of the actions they undertake are subordinated to their political survival or promotion. As explained by the theory, this is normally conducive to ever growing public sectors, which finally become oversized and inefficient.

2.2.1. *The debate on growing transfers and reduction of taxes*

In the context of the theory of Public Choice and derivatives, the most scrutinised and criticised expenditures of public budgets have been, and are, the so-called "social transfers" (pensions, subsidies to unemployed and other social benefits). Up to the 70s these expenditures grew steadily in many Western countries. However, economic analysis[34] had already proven that many of these expenditures, as then devised, contained some disincentives for activity. In particular we could mention unemployment subsidies for long lasting periods; indiscriminate financing of the health system irrespective of the contributions of the individuals; the setting up of excessively generous pensions not related to contributions; and other programmes directed to welfare sharing.

To sustain a growing level of public activities, it was necessary to count with a parallel volume of public revenues, mainly taxes. One of these, the income tax, being progressive and with high marginal rates, had in some Western countries started to choke the initiative of quite a number of individuals. It also became clear that politicians and parliaments could not indefinitely expand the rates of the taxes without putting the consolidated revenues at risk. Indeed it is not difficult to prove that for any taxed good or service, from a certain level onwards, an increase of rates is conducive to a reduction of the correspondent revenue.

This correct microeconomic idea, transplanted to macro-economics, supported the convenience of reducing the current tax rates in order to increase the revenues of Western governments, as predicted by the so-called Laffer curve[35]. Unfortunately this practise

---

34. Okun, A. (1975) "Equality and Efficiency: the big trade off". Brookings Institution.

35. It is well acknowledged that the existence of marginal rates of income tax, placed around 80% in the highest slab of income, have ruined for years many attempts of personal initiative of the citizens in countries that have adopted this policy (except in the case of generalised dodging the taxman).

had an adverse effect in many cases, increasing public deficits instead of reducing them. This happened as a result of the non-linear mathematical relation between rates and revenues, and due to the fact that at the time of implementation the fiscal position of the involved countries was not in the profitable segment of the curve.

2.3. Models in competence: the triumph of the neo-classical model

For more than a century, two economic models were in competence for explaining the economic behaviour of the agents: the Marxist and the Neo-classical one. The Marxist explanation of the long-term non-viability of capitalism was based on its purported contradictions. In order to explain its non-sustainability, Marxist analysis focussed on private owners of capital goods, who in their industrial relations with workers obtained a surplus, depriving the employed masses of part of the value generated by them (rate of exploitation). According to Marx, these internal contradictions would historically produce progressive discontentment among workers and ever growing economic cycles, resulting in the crumbling of capitalism and its substitution by socialism, followed finally by communism.

The economics of Marx was essentially a dynamic theory, partially based on the classical value of labour (Smith and Ricardo), with contemporary components of sociology and politics, capable of inducing a theory of the organisation of the production in stages. In the stage of socialism, the former production based on free markets and on the exploitation of workers would disappear, and would be substituted by the socialisation of assets of production.

It was with the implementation of Marxist economy that economic planning emerged[36]. The need of establishing prices for goods and salaries and the required mutual consistency of the different industrial productions forced the appearance of central planning. An approach that, lacking the flexibility of decentralised markets became more and more untenable when the number of goods to be produced increased along the economic development

---

36. After the Russian revolution in 1917, the revolutionaries needed several years to develop a central planning strategy in order to make the model operative.

process. Gradually it became clear that this approach also lacked the necessary stimuli for increasing productivity, private saving and for timely taking new economic initiatives, thus being condemned to perpetual inefficiency.

2.3.1. Rise and decline of Keynesian economics

The Great Depression of the 30s seemed to prelude the end of capitalism as predicted by Marx. However, capitalism of those days found in the weapons industry and in the ideas of J.M. Keynes, based on partial intervention of the state, means to compensate the lack of private demand. The Keynesian system, a mix of free market economy and juncture state interventions, later on complemented with the implementation of welfare economics and the development of the welfare state, generated a growth of public sectors.

Unfortunately, the Keynesian model, as explained by Keynesians[37] and Monetarists, contained certain areas of in-definition, particularly in relation to the long-term effects of the public deficits on inflation, when they are monetizised. On the other hand, initially recommended increases in public expenditure by naïve Keynesians, paid practically no attention to its efficiency, since it was thought that efficient or less efficient increases in public expenditure were a better solution than no increase in public demand at all.

The historical application of the Keynesian model by Western governments contained an additional flaw: the propensity of politicians to increase expenditure in times of slowdown or depression, and to increase taxes in moments of buoyancy or faster price-rises, thus supporting a continued growth of public sectors over the business cycle.

In many cases, the indefinite and reckless succession of deficits provoked the increase of internal outstanding public debt in terms of GDP, limiting future application of this kind of policy when necessary.

Summing up, one could say that the imprudent application of the Keynesian recipes by politicians finally drove this policy to a blind

---

37. A significant part of macroeconomists have differentiated between the Economics of Keynes and the Keynesian Economics, as practised from 50s to 70s. Leiyonhufvud, A. (1965) The Keynesian Economics and the Economics of Keynes.

alley. The more the above mentioned dysfunction became clear, criticism to public intervention started gaining ground. The critics came from different groups of theorists, all of them belonging to the most liberal tradition. Some pioneers among them, the so called "Monetarists" already in the 60s criticised economic activism of governments, because of its pro-cyclical inconvenience, and the oblivion of its inflationary effects.

2.3.2. *Return to neo-classicism*

Years later, the "new neo-classical economists" built a new micro-acro model that once more condemned the occasional political interventions of the state for its ineffectiveness, as they were convinced that the market system guaranteed a steady growth in equilibrium. A third group, the "theorists of the Public Choice", attacked the ever growing public sectors arguing that its development was mainly due to the personal interest of politicians and bureaucrats, and not so much to the real interests of the society.

As a consequence the pendulum started moving to the other side. In those days, supporters of this movement, far from attacking only the ineffective public interventions (such as some subsidies to production or consumption, the continuation of non strategic public firms, or the direct interventions in financial or real markets), attacked almost the entire public sector. They even put into question the convenience of keeping services such as health, education, pensions, and provision of some infrastructures and others, inside the public sector. Following the appearance of new technologies, the provision of goods and services that for long had been considered a matter of natural public monopolies (railways, telephones, electricity, water) was also put into question.

Leaving aside these pendulum movements, and in conclusion, we have to say that nowadays there is only one valid model for understanding the functioning of the economy, and that this model allows for a variable degree of public intervention or production of goods and services. In other words: in any economy most of the interchanges should work according to the principles of competence, and the rest should work under direct or indirect interventions of public powers.

2.4. The neo-classical model and the law of pendulum

From a practical point of view, the relative abandonment of Keynesianism as the foundation of applied policies was considered valid in the economic context of the 70s. Let us remember that in the 70s the Bretton Woods system of fixed exchange rates had crumbled, and a sudden multiplication of oil prices with high potential for inflationary acceleration had appeared onto the scene. Some years after the first oil crisis, it was thought that an adjustment to high rates of oil price increases would change into a galloping inflation, which could jeopardise the political and social order in Western countries[38]. Hence the urgency in those days to fight against inflation.

On the other hand, the then more prone defenders[39] of the market economy proclaimed the convenience of recovering the full freedom of markets, distorted by previous exaggerated micro and macro interventionism which allegedly had generated unemployment[40]. They based their ideas on the assumptions that prices and wages were flexible and that the economic agents would always use all the available information to anticipate government actions.

One has to admit that some of these assumptions and related new approaches were valid, and that they have replaced the old ones[41]. Others however were clearly biased and unrealistic (for instance the assumption that the fast clearance of all markets, based on the flexibility of prices and wages, would quickly result in full

---

38. Maddison, A. (2001: 131). The world economy: A millennium perspective. OECD, Paris.

39. Among these economists we could mention the Nobel-awarded Lucas, R. and Sargent, T. In their publication "After Keynesian Macroeconomics" they explained that "existing Keynesian macroeconomic models cannot provide reliable guidance in the formulation of monetary, fiscal or other types of policy... There is no hope that minor or even major modifications of these models will lead to significant improvement in their reliability." Also the contributions of Wallace, N. and Barro, R., were relevant in the restatement of the neo-classical model.

40. The reality however has proved the opposite. The rate of unemployment steadily grew in the periods 1974-1983, 1984-1993 and 1994-1998 practically everywhere. Although in the US the rate of unemployment fell from 1984 onwards, its current rate in 2003 is over the average of the period 1950-1973, the era of interventionism. Maddison, A. (2001: 134), book already mentioned.

41. For instance the replacement of backward looking "adaptive expectations" for new forward looking "rational expectations".

employment). Based on these assumptions a new mathematically elegant economic model was built. According to this model, systematic fiscal and monetary policies were irrelevant for combating unemployment. Notwithstanding the weakness of one of its basic assumptions (the flexibility of prices and wages) the new neo-classical economic model and its policy derivatives quickly gained ground and came into the forefront, calling for liberalisation of markets, zero inflation target[42] and downsizing of the public sector.

2.4.1 The Thatcher-Reagan experiment

Against this doubtful intellectual background, complemented with some ultra classical ideas in the field of public finance (supply-side economics), which to some extent were simple derivatives of the struggle for life in the academic world, two governments decided to put this new recipe into practise. In the early 80s Margaret Thatcher (UK) and Ronald Reagan (US), sticking to the new interpretations of the working of the market economy, took the first steps to hastily correct the somewhat oversized public sector and to facilitate the clearance of markets. They started a de-escalation of the degree of intervention in private markets, and a rushed privatisation of public firms and some services, disregarding further problems of industrial concentration and income distribution. In parallel they implemented tax reductions in line with the Laffer recommendations, and severe monetary corrections to choke the existing inflation [43].

Letting aside some doubts on the global validity of this approach, two external and independent developments seemed to support the assumed success. First, the economic recovery that started in the West in 1983-84 appeared as very strong after a long period of standstill, apparently validating the new economic approach. Second, the crumbling of the Marxist founded planning system of extreme public intervention, as practised by the Soviet

---

42. Only two decades later, this recommended optimum zero inflation target became a serious concern for mainstream economists. This is because this target can provoke a problem much more dangerous than that of inflation: the deflation of prices conducive to depression or stagnation, as it has recently been the case in Japan.

43. We should not forget that in parallel with tax reductions, Reagan significantly increased the US defence expenditure (in particular to finance the so-called Stars War) which was conducive to a huge public deficit, against recommended by new neo-classicals.

Union and satellites, additionally seemed to confirm the supremacy of the new approach as the only way to produce a steady and generalised growth process.

This new economic policy, quickly spread to many countries of the world, and also impregnated the philosophy of the Bretton Woods institutions devoted to assessing policies and financing external deficits and development. In particular, outward oriented policies were indiscriminately and hastily promoted within the so-called Structural Adjustment Programmes. Paradoxically, and against the basic political corollaries deriving from the model, the accessibility to agriculture and services markets of Western countries by LDC, as well as freer movements of labour, remained denied.

2.4.2. *An approach to the model with doubtful results*

In order to provisionally assess the working of the above-mentioned approach, we could take a closer look into the economic and social results of leading countries that have implemented this policy. First of all, one should consider that the rate of unemployment in all Western countries, including the US, has been on an average higher in the booming period 1983-98 than in the period 1950-1973. On the other hand, the implicit pledges of generalised prosperity stemming from the undertaken approach were not met in many places[44]. The internal distribution of income also suffered, unleashing more violence and crime[45]. In the international context, the increase in the regional economic gap of the last 20 years could be another proof of the long-term deficiency of the chosen approach.

In conclusion we could say that, even without rejecting some undeniable advances of this new economic policy, be these internal or external, the new approach accumulated meaningful weaknesses. One of these weaknesses has been the indiscriminate degrading of the regime (amount and accessibility) of social transfers. Note that in the name of their former inefficiency, some transfers underwent exaggerated reductions at national and international level, with negative results for global growth and the fight against poverty.

---

44. See note number 17, Chapter 1.

45. Note the relevance of these phenomena in the US where, in the name of freedom, a high percentage of citizens have to be kept behind bars.

We could also say that as a result of the generalised privatisation movement, industrial concentration at national and international level has further increased, to the demerit of consumers and the distribution of income. The pendulum, as normally happens, has moved again. This time from the naïve and recklessly applied Keynesian policies in the 60s and early 70s, to a purported extreme market liberalisation with oblivion, and sometimes contempt of some vital public sector interventions.

2.5. Wrong international application of the neo-classical model

Letting aside theoretical discussions on the optimum position of the pendulum, we have to say that the desirable composition of the private and public sectors in every economy, to some extent depends on the degree of development[46], and is not exclusively an issue of political evaluation and choice[47]. It is also important to note that the current mainstream approach tends to forget some relevant corollaries or outcomes, belonging to the background of the neo-classical theory, or tends to keep important lacunae in implementation.

A good example of this double standard is that related to the pressure of Western countries for liberalisation of capital movements in developing countries, while at the same time the West refuses to open their labour markets even minimally to developing countries. This double standard is often disguised with pure semantics. A good example of this can be found in the WTO negotiations, where alternative proposals or limitations introduced by LDC are openly disdained as "ideology" by negotiators from rich countries. At the same time Western countries defend their own proposed limitations

---

46. Note that the different stages of the development of countries condition the size of the public sector. This is because the fiscal burden cannot be high in a LDC, since the public sector cannot raise relevant amounts of taxes from the poor majorities. At the same time, even if (improbably) the rich minority (often in power) was overtaxed, the necessary amounts for a balanced financing of public goods would not be met. Needless to say that, world wide, the rich are not keen on fiscal reforms to increase the financial capabilities of the public sector.

47. Between conventional public agencies and private corporations, there are a number of organisational forms that may be able to achieve many of the efficiency benefits of private organisations, while at the same time pursue public interests more effectively than a purely private firm subject to regulations. Stiglitz, J. (2000: 211), book already mentioned.

as just "technical restrictions" imposed (exclusively) by the legal framework of their countries.

2.5.1. *Lack of knowledge on optimisation during economic transition*

Entering into details, one should not forget that although the neo-classical model is pretty well formulated in static terms, its dynamics are not so well understood. Economists know quite well the traits of steady growth of competitive economies that start from a balanced position of markets and sectors and continue in it, or the optimal paths to move from one economic structure to another, in the framework of planning. However, economists have no clear ideas about the optimal path or temporal dimensions of a move from a (partial) non-competitive situation to a (complete) competitive one. The Russian experience is a striking case of the consequences of this lack of ideas, described also by Stiglitz[48].

Following recommendations of the IMF, the Russian transition from a mainly non-competitive to a competitive economy was a dangerous mix of hasty privatisation, liberalisation and decentralisation, implemented along a period of international recession. This was too stodgy for Russian economic agents, who as others, were in need of phasing periods for each of these corrections. Without implementing a rational phasing the result was a chaos, in which a selective group of cronies took advantage of hasty liberalisation, stripping state property with pure speculative ends[49].

Theoretically we could say that a fast liberalisation of markets would be correct if suddenly, in a fraction of a second, all the markets changed from a situation of controlled prices or quantities, or both of them, to that of competitive flexible prices. Unfortunately reality does not work like that since some relevant markets (such as labour markets, protected agriculture and industrial markets) contain enormous doses of inertia, and their agents are often reluctant to adjust quickly.

Consequently, transplanting the economic recipes for gaining efficiency, supplied by the static neo-classical model in order to fall

---

48. Stiglitz, J. (2002: 151). Globalisation and its discontent, book already mentioned.
49. Stiglitz, J. (2002: 133).

within a dynamic framework, may generate non-optimal solutions. For instance a sudden liberalisation of the labour market is often conducive to strikes that not only may disrupt this market but also the rest. Likewise a sudden liberalisation or an instant abatement of tariff duties in international trade may disrupt a relevant part of the industrial production of developing countries. Thus a sensible solution would be gradualism or the establishment of phasing out periods.

Having said this, we have to underline that, from an empirical point of view the interpretation of every specific process of phasing has historically been different in every market and in every country.

2.5.2. *On the problem of the second best*

Another problem usually contained in some static recipes extracted from the neo-classical model is the oblivion of the so-called "second best"[50] problem. Over a long period, the neo-classical economists thought that if for any reason one of the conditions for optimality was not fulfilled, it was still desirable and recommendable to fulfil the rest in order to reach an attainable optimum, of course inferior to *optimum optimorum*. Today, however, this approach of "optimising the possible" is in some relevant cases considered wrong by the doctrine.

From a practical point of view this means that, if in an economy several markets start being liberalised and others are not, there is no guarantee that the final situation will be better (from the perspective of general welfare) than the former one. A typical example of the "second best" problem is the recently world-wide generalised internal liberalisation of capital markets, while at the same time the internal labour markets have remained in a non-competitive position. In this case the price of labour will be higher than that of its competitive position, while the interest rates will result competitive, that is to say effectively lower than before[51].

---

50. Lipsey, R.G. and Lancaster, K. "The General Theory of the Second Best" in Farrel, M.G. (1973) Readings in Welfare Economics.

51. Note that in many countries of the world, although the governments had for long established nominal ceilings to interest rates under those of equilibrium, the effective rates finally paid by borrowers have been much higher than those derived from alternative competitive situations. Vide the Mac-Kinnon and Shaw model. A simple version of this model can be seen in Frey, M.(1978) "Money and capital financing deepening in economic development" in Journal of Money, Credit and Banking. November 1978.

Consequently, if the price of labour unduly maintains its level and the price of capital decreases, a process of substitution of labour by capital is expectable, which could increase the implicit or explicit rate of unemployment.

The above-mentioned negative case of internal lack of simultaneity of liberalisation of capital and labour markets could also be applied at an international level. This is because the different national labour markets have continued being segmented, while the free movements of capital have become a constant in the context of contemporary globalisation. Logically, to be consistent with the alleged pro-competitive targets of Western countries, following the corollaries of the neo-classical model, liberalisation of international movements of people should have been undertaken. Regrettably, this has not been the case, thus reducing the total rate of employment at a world scale. In brief, Western countries have also in this case shown a non-competitive behaviour against the goodness of competitive markets constantly heralded by them.

2.5.3. *Necessary and sufficient conditions for optimising*

It is very common in economic discussions to confuse the necessary conditions to achieve a result with the sufficient conditions. Many misunderstandings emerge in negotiations when one side affirms that one condition is necessary to obtain a determined outcome, while the other denies its sufficiency, both of them believing that the conditions defended by either side are in contradiction with each other, when both sides may be right or wrong[52].

For instance in the current discussions on the development of LDC, the so-called Washington Consensus proclaim several conditions (as described in note 2) as necessary conditions for development. However a number of concerned governments of LDC argue that the fulfilment of some of these conditions is neither necessary nor sufficient for economic progress. In this regard, concerned LDC governments often reject hasty liberalisation of internal and external markets, as a necessary condition to boost development. Paradoxically, many Europeans who nowadays defend

---

52. Lipsey, R.G. (1984: Apend. A.) "Introduction to Positive Economics".

the conditions of the Washington Consensus fail to remember the economic history of Europe, which in the 60s developed at fast track without fulfilling many of these "necessary" conditions.

In abstract terms, one could conceive a quick development of a country or a group of countries, without the existence of generalised free markets. On the other hand, the existence of free markets cannot guarantee steady growth, if at the same time the process of investments stagnate due to a lack of financing. In this last case the existence of free markets would neither be a sufficient condition nor a necessary one, while an appropriate rate of investment[53] would be necessary.

Nevertheless implementers of the Washington Consensus consider that these conditions are not only necessary but also sufficient. In their view, any LDC that wants to promote its economy will need to meet these conditions. Thereafter automatically increased domestic savings will finance higher rates of domestic investment; FDI will significantly flow in; and a sustained growth path will naturally be established.

Conversely other economists express concern that many LDC may have only a limited ability to increase internal savings to attract FDI, and to create sufficient domestic investments, even after fulfilling the Washington Consensus conditions[54].

Hence it is clear that general recipes as proposed by the Washington Consensus cannot be applied for all countries in all circumstances. The experience with the geographical distribution of FDI across LDC through the last decade proves that many countries cannot attract FDI due to difficulties in their location, the small size of their economies and the lack of natural and human resources and poor infrastructure, although they have acceptable governance.

Consequently, the implementation of the Washington Consensus reforms in these LDC will not necessary speed up development, will

---

53. Rostow, W. (1960) in "The Stages of Economic Growth", Cambridge University Press, pointed out that one of the necessary conditions for the taking off of a LDC is the attainment of a significant jump in the investment rate, which should be placed above 15% in terms of GDP. According to the economic history we know that the countries that have quickly caught up (Japan, Asian tigers, etc) have experienced domestic investment rates of around or more than 30%.

54. Lipsey, R.G. and Chrystal, K.A. (1999: 574). "Principles of Economics". Oxford University Press.

neither attract sufficient FDI, nor will it significantly boost internal savings to finance greater domestic investments. We could add to this that the generalised recommendation of hastily opening to imports of internal markets in LDC is also contrary to the own experience of the Western countries. These countries, including US, EU, Japan (as well as the NICs) gradually phased and differentiated the opening of their internal markets along the history of their industrialisation.

2.6. Selfish interpretations of neo-classicism by the West

In economic negotiations, the stronger party normally imposes criteria, which favours its own interest. Clear examples of these uneven results in international negotiations in the past decades have been 1) the development of an asymmetric and unbalanced liberalisation of international trade; and 2) the non-development of an international labour market. Note that both aspects are against the corollaries of the competitive model and, consequently, against the principle of increasing the welfare of the global society.

2.6.1. *Asymmetric liberalisation of international trade: growing gap*

As mentioned before, one of the necessary conditions for taking off, or for steady growth at rhythms of catching up in LDC, is to count with a sufficient volume of internal or external savings to finance the required higher domestic investments. Since internally available funds are usually insufficient, the reception of foreign funds emerges as a necessary and complementary condition for growth. At the same time, the reception of these foreign funds enables LDC to balance their deficits on the current account.

Logically, if exports of LDC grow fast, *ceteris paribus*, the need to resort to foreign or external savings will decrease. Consequently, as foreign funds and exports are to some extent substitutes, the latter should be enhanced according to the principle of comparative advantage. On the other hand rich countries should not hinder the exports of developing countries, if they effectively want to promote efficiency, as stemming from the neo-classical model.

It is a fact that in the 60s and in the first half of the 70s the growth rates of global production and global trade increased significantly, and almost all the countries, developing and developed ones, profited from this prosperity. Nevertheless, if we consider the period 1970-2001 and we focus on developing countries (including central planned economies and their successors), we find that the share of the exports originating from these countries have fluctuated at around 25% of global exports[55].

Even worse, although the global relation of trade to GDP rose in the considered period, this ratio fell for the 44 LDC. All this signifies that, from the perspective of international trade, many non-rich countries did not experience any relative improvement in their commercial position, despite successive multilateral negotiations (GATT and WTO) on reductions of tariffs and other barriers to trade.

Nevertheless, in the name of reaching market efficiency and boosting development of developing countries, the Western countries are constantly putting pressure on the latter to haste reduction of their protectionism[56]. This pressure is exerted mainly in the field of industrial products, while the West comfortably keeps a difficult access to its internal markets of agricultural goods and services.

It is time to recognise that today's pro-open-market hype is an asymmetric and unbalanced approach for the development of LDC and a forgetful reading of history. First it ignores the own very high protectionism of the Western countries in the earlier stages of their development. And second, it forgets the significant transfers of funds from the colonies towards the colonising powers[57] in exchange for practically nothing.

---

55. Todaro, M. (2000: 461). Economic Development. 7th Ed. Longman. Pearson Education. Vide Also World Bank (2003: 314). "03 World Development Indicators". From this last source one may deduce that the share in 2001 of low and middle income countries reached the figure of 24.7%.

56. We firmly believe that although positive, a quick integration of developing countries into the world economy is not so powerful a force of growth as the Washington Consensus considers. As it has happened historically inside developed countries, free internal trade among internal regions has not guaranteed catching up growth to all regions. To pursue this target, these countries were forced to implement a policy of relevant public transfers to backward regions, and to encourage internal migrations.

57. Just to put examples, we could mention the case of the Netherlands that extracted annually from Indonesia up to 8% of the Netherlands GDP in those days. On the other hand, although UK had established a free trade system after the abolition of the East Indian Company in 1857, its external economic policies were accompanied by hangovers from mercantilism. British shipping, banking and insurance interests enjoyed a de facto monopoly (...), which was reinforced by lack of education of the native population. Maddison, A (1989), The World Economy in the 20th Century. OECD, Paris.

In our days the rich countries continue to keep high tariffs, so-called "tariff peaks", that also restrict imports from LDC. Additionally, high subsidies on agriculture, and the introduction of other non-tariff barriers that restrict commerce, as for instance food safety standards often more restricted than internationally recommended, are all aspects of this renewed protectionism. This puts into question the Western intentions in promoting an efficient global economic system in line with the neo-classical approach.

In the words of Nicholas Stern of the World Bank[58], "it is surely hypocritical of rich countries to encourage LDC to liberalise trade and to tackle the associated problems of adjustment, whilst at the same time succumbing to powerful groups in their own interest that seek to perpetuate protection of the narrow self interest."

It is alarming, and in the long term even against own interest, that in international negotiations (WTO) the Western countries insist that they will not abate the mentioned agriculture barriers if the other side does not do the same with industrial products. This is at least a position that, although based on a second best criterion between equals, ignores any historical debt and hinders a faster development of LDC, necessary for their catching up in a reasonable time span. Even more, recent internal concessions of Western governments to their farming constituencies[59], establishing long time spans for abatement, have created an inflexible frame that hinders any significant progress in this field in the coming decade.

Figures presented by Stern[60] clarify that the potential welfare (real income) gains from further global trade policy reforms are very large. Specifically developing countries could gain annually around US $ 75 billion dollars from liberalisation of merchandise trade by OECD

---

58. Stern, N. (2001: 8) Globalisation, the Investment Climate, and Poverty Reduction. Indian Council for Research on International Economic Relations. New Delhi.

59. Note that in 2002, the US with its Farm Bill and the EU with the Franco-German agreement on EU farm support, have clearly stepped backward in "their proclaimed" long march towards efficiency in global markets. Nonetheless recently the EU has modified its Common Agriculture Policy (CAP), allegedly to decouple subsidies and prices, although the scope of the modifications is limited in the short-term.

60. Stern, N. (2002: 10) Making Trade Work for Poor People. National Council of Applied Economic Research, New Delhi.

countries. A gain that clearly exceeds the meagre ODA received, currently placed around US 50 billion dollars per annum, which means that the current ODA is not a net aid since it only partially offsets the damage caused by protectionism practised by the industrialised countries.

Although the Western countries used to show off on their average tariffs of less than 5% on industrial products, even today these countries continue keeping high tariff duties on relevant export goods from LDC, in particular for agricultural products, textiles and clothing. According to Stern, on an average the highest tariffs charged are 40 times the ruling average in the OECD countries. Summing up, the above-mentioned trade positions of rich countries are against the principle of comparative advantage, against the heralded pursue of international efficiency, and against historical equity.

2.6.2. The labour market: a non-considered step for efficient globalisation

As mentioned above, according to the theory of the second best, it is at least doubtful that liberalising one market or a group of them, without liberalising the rest, is conducive to a global increase in economic welfare. It is also well known that liberalisation applied to the movement of capital gathered momentum mainly along the 90s. However the different national labour markets remain segmented, thus avoiding pooling of different supplies and demands of every labour speciality that meaningfully could increase global welfare and employment.

As it is easily deducible, from a "static point of view"[61] and in a context of pure competence, the merger of previously segmented labour markets, with different functions of demand and supply, and different wages in every segmented market, will generate a unique wage, thus benefiting the global economic welfare. Concentrating on the sub-effects of this static global gain, we can say that suppliers to the market with lower initial wages (workers of LDC), and market demanders with higher previous wages (firms of rich countries) will gain. Meanwhile the suppliers to the market with

---

61. Samuelson, P. and Nordhaus, W. (1998: 241) Economics. Mc Graw-Hill. New York.

initial higher wages (workers of developed countries), and the demanders in the market with initially lower wages (firms of LDC) will lose. This means that the wages in markets with initial high salaries, like those in the OECD countries, would experience a reduction, while the wages in markets with initial lower salaries, like those of LDC, would register an increase. And all this would be parallel to a flow of workers from the second market to the first one.

To the extent that the new wages in the rich countries would be lower than before, the techniques of production would become less intensive in capital. This would relatively reduce the internal demand of capital in these countries, which would induce a reduction in real interest rates. Conversely in LDC the newly increased wages would provoke a relative increase in the demand of capital, a movement that would bring an increase of real interest rates. These effects of liberalisation of labour markets would consequently induce (if authorised) an additional movement of capital from the rich countries towards the poor ones.

Summing up, we could say that, on the one hand the rich countries are pressing LDC for additional liberalisation of their capital inflows, in order to fulfil one of the "necessary conditions" of the Washington Consensus. On the other, they surprisingly move in opposite direction avoiding a sure and relevant flow of capital to LDC by means of impeding a parallel liberalisation and de-segmentation of their own labour markets.

This asymmetry in the liberalisation of the various factor markets is once again an example of the underlying political restrictions in rich countries, that forces an undesirable application of one of the main corollaries of the neo-classical model. In this regard it is also paradoxical that while internally the rich countries push for geographical mobility of labour in the name of market efficiency, externally they reject this mobility[62]. Although we understand the high political sensitivity of this issue in rich countries, what cannot

---

62. Normally, when LDC pose this problem in international negotiations against own concessions in trade, the Western countries divert this discussion to the International Labour Organisation. And they do this as if the underlying problem was theoretically different from that of the freedom in the movements of capital that rich countries constantly defend within WTO.

be understood is the asymmetry in the underlying arguments used in international negotiations in the name of global competition.

Chart 1

*Net migration in the donor countries, 1870-1998
(in miles; negative sign implies outflow)*

	1870-1913	1914-49	1950-73	1974-98
France	890	-236	3630	1026
France	890	-236	3630	1026
Germany	-2598	-304	7070	5911
Italy	-4459	-1771	-2139	1617
UK	-6415	-1405	-605	737
Total West Europe	-13996	-3662	9381	10898
Japan	n.a.	197	-72	-179
Australia	885	673	2033	2151
New Zealand	290	138	247	87
Canada	861	207	2126	2680
US	15820	6221	8257	16721
Total EIC group	17856	7239	12663	21639

Source: Maddison, A.(2001:128), book already mentioned.

In the context of the theoretical convenience of liberalisation of the labour movements, it is interesting to keep in mind the international migration flows that occurred between 1950 and 1998. In this post-war era, the Western European countries have approximately received 20 million immigrants, while the so-called "European Immigration Countries"[63] received 34 million. However, rich countries have not always received a net migration. Note that the trend changed its sign in the second half of the 20th century. While between 1870 and 1949 there was an exodus of European people who tried to improve their poor living conditions by moving abroad, since 1950 Western European countries approximately received 20 million immigrants, mainly from Mediterranean and other developing countries.

---

63. This group of "European Immigration Countries" includes Australia, New Zealand, Canada and the US. Vide Chart 1 taken from Maddison, A. (2001:128), book already mentioned.

Concerning Europe, we have to say that the 20 million immigrants received in a period of 48 years represent a magnitude of around 4,00,000 per annum, a figure which is near 0.13% of the current European population. These immigrants are mainly based in selected European countries, and particularly in some cities. Although their concentration has increased the visibility of immigrants, they have scantly contributed to the allegedly desired higher growth of Western European population[64]. Note that the European population only grew at around 0.5% annually during the second half of the 20th century. This small figure of 0.5%, well under the population growth registered in the rest of the rich world, has contributed in the last two decades to the population ageing, to the lower growth rate of the European labour-force and GDP, and to the growing EU-US GDP gap in the past 20 years[65].

2.7. Inefficient application of the neo-classical model

As we have described above, the neo-classical model is clearly superior to its alternative. But to arrive at efficient outcomes, the model should at least be corrected of its market failures (lack of competition, public goods, externalities, and so on). The absence of these corrections, or the ignorance of some of its corollaries, may generate incorrect interpretations of the model as well as wrong applications. In the past two decades the wrong applications by Western and developing countries have induced breakdowns and unexpected outcomes. No wonder that the selected approach did not result in economic catching up of LDC in this period.

Although both sides may have committed some mistakes, the responsibility for the failures and negative outcomes has been mostly on the side of the Western countries. Unfortunately for all players, rich countries, despite constantly invoking the principles of market freedom, have pushed for an *ad hoc* economic aperture, imposing a

---

64. The desirable rate of growth of Western European population should be higher than the current one to solve problems of ageing and financing of pensions. In this regard the figures of the US in the same period, with a growth rate of around 1%, are more promising.

65. However in recent days, rich countries are starting to acknowledge the vital role that immigration could play in their economies, not in the least in relation to their deficient population growth and ill population pyramids. WB. Press Review 26-11-03.

defective and sometimes quick[66] selection of the markets to be liberalised. The exclusion of the labour market from liberalisation is the most striking example of the inconsistency of the approach followed[67].

It is clear that the developing countries could have increased their international trade also by means of creation of additional (regional) trade blocs, thus reducing trade barriers with neighbouring countries[68]. Note however that the errors accumulated by Western countries in trade and other issues have been much more significant, and in the long run even against their own interest.

The managing of global sustainability (emissions, earth warming, correction of externalities, etc), indispensable for the working of the model in the long term, has not significantly been pursued by the North, while this part of the world has historically been the one mainly responsible for emissions and earth warming.

A correct working of the model also requires good governance. This is essential to properly manage the public sector and efficiently correct externalities. This is also necessary to achieve, among other things, the so-called "good economic environment" (the fight against corruption, stability of economic rules including taxes and contracting, etc.). But good governance as currently understood by the Washington Consensus (forcing quick public sector down scaling, privatisation, and hasty liberalisation etc.) may result in more concentration and less competition in demerit of consumers.

---

66. The case of Russia and many of its former satellites illustrates the irrationality of sudden changes in the organisation of the markets. This mistake has for long been conducive to reductions of GDP in these countries. It is not credible, in strict economic sense, that the IMF forced this policy as a condition for loans to avoid Russian bankruptcy, when this condition practically guarantied the disruption of Russian economy.

67. Some economists or politicians could consider the international liberalisation of this market as something idealistic or utopia. But the lack of introduction of this "idealistic" corollary can turn (according the Theory of the Second Best) the liberalisation of others into non-positive. "The Economist" (2003: 49) February 1st-7th.

68. Note that in the 90s, with the exception of the high income economies and the regions Middle-East and North Africa, all the regions of the planet have experienced growth rates of their regional exports (to other countries of the same region) significantly larger than the world average (5.8%). In particular the annual growth rate of exports to countries of the same region has peaked in the region Eastern Asia-Pacific (17%). World Bank (2003: 315) "03 World Development Indicators".

We do believe that, given the current failures of markets and the new tempo of history, the Western countries should devote more efforts to support further gradual reform processes in developing countries and a better sequencing[69] of applied policies. At the same time they should speed up the dismantling of their own trade barriers in relation with exports of developing countries, and boost and pool funds for reaching international public goods.

---

69. As to sequencing, experience has confirmed that private capital will only flow to areas with likely high returns. No wonder that private capital flows (mainly FDI) towards developing countries, have bypassed LDC, due to the lack of infrastructures, energy and human capital of the latter. Given also that these countries cannot resort to sufficient internal savings to finance the former mentioned public goods, the only available solution they have is to resort to external public financing.

3

Economic Results of Globalisation and the Role of the Multilateral Institutions

To correctly assess the effective incidence of the different applied economic models (Keynesian, socialist, neo-classical), we will look into the evolution of the macroeconomic performance across the world in the period 1950-1998. Additionally when convenient, we will also refer to the figures of the period 1870-1913, the so-called period of "liberal order"[70]. To analyse the period 1950-1998, we have divided it in two sub-periods: 1) the period of generalised and growing prosperity, 1950-1973, also called "the golden age" of capitalism; and 2) the "neo-liberal period" which extended from 1973 to 1998.

Note that the analysis will be made in very aggregated terms. Although this could hide interesting details concerning certain prominent countries, it will not contradict the general trends in the different regions of the world. When convenient we will make special reference to some countries (Arab-Muslim countries and EU zone) and focus on the last two decades, a period that practically coincides with the above-defined "neo-liberal era". To have a deeper understanding of the global economic evolution, we will also look into the policies of international economic institutions, the Bretton Woods institutions (World Bank and IMF) and WTO as successor of GATT.

3.1. Trends of the world economy in the period 1950-1998

It is beyond any doubt that in the second half of the 20th century, the world economy has obtained its best ever results. According to

---

70. Note that this "liberal order" mainly referred to a selected group countries in the world. This order was led by mainland of the British Empire.

a recent research[71], the global GDP grew at an average growth rate of 3.9% per annum, compared to a growth rate of 1.6% per annum in the period 1820-1950. Another indicator of buoyancy of the second half of the 20th Century, is that the average annual per capita growth rate in this period was 2.1% against 0.9% between 1820 and 1950. This means that in the second half of the 20th century, the global per capita GDP has grown to a rhythm that allowed doubling the global standard of living every 35 years, as compared to the time frame of 80 years that was necessary during the period 1820-1950.

3.1.1. Evolution of GDP in the world

The former figure of 3.9% of the GDP growth in 1950-1998, is the weighted average of that of the "golden age of capitalism" (1950-1973), and that of the period of "neo-liberalism" (1973-1998). Note that in the golden age the per capita GDP in the world grew at a rate of almost 3% per annum. The greatest ever in history.

Entering now into details of the golden age, we will mention that the growth rate of Japan was the most remarkable (9.29%). Against what one could have imagined, the European Immigration Countries (US, Canada, Australia and New Zealand, hereafter referred to as EIC group) experienced the lowest GDP growth rate (4.03%) of all regions[72], even below Africa (4.45%), Western Europe (4.81%), USSR and satellites (4.84%), Asia ex-Japan (5.18%), and Latin America (5.33%).

Regarding the neo-liberal period, in which the global GDP growth rate per annum was 3.01%, that is to say around 3/5 of that of the golden age, we should note the remarkable disintegration of Eastern Europe, with its growth rate going into negative (-0.56%) from

---

71. Maddison, A. (2001: 125), book already mentioned. The periods selected by Maddison are arbitrary and consequently arguable. However we will not enter in discussions on this issue because identifying periods is mainly a matter of historians, and because any other arbitrary selection would not modify the results significantly.

72. It is convenient to remember that the 50s were a decade of slow growth for the US, a country that was forced to change the structure of its economy, until then significantly focussed on the production of weaponry. With the arrival of the Democrats in 1960, US started the practise of an ultra Keynesian policy in the American economy, which was called "the new frontier economics". This policy, accompanied by the escalation of the Vietnam conflict, accelerated the growth rate of the US and reduced the unemployment rate, although at the cost of an increased inflation rate.

earlier 4.84%. Also Japan decelerated its previous spectacular rhythm of growth, converging to the average growth rate of the world. Note additionally that while Western Europe had annually grown in the golden age almost 1 percent point above the EIC, the situation overturned in the neo-liberal period, with the EIC growing almost 1 percent point more than Western Europe.

Significantly above the world average, the Asian (ex-Japan) countries not only maintained the growth rate of that of the golden age (5.18%), but also surpassed it (5.46%)[73], this figure being almost twofold of the world average. No doubt, this period (1973-1998) of general decline in global growth was the period of the economic resurgence of Asia, commanded by a vanguard group of 7 fast growing countries.

3.1.2. *Evolution of world population*

To continue with our aggregated analysis, we will now focus on the evolution of demography in the periods 1950-1973, the golden age, and 1973-1998, the neo-liberal period. We can see in Chart 2, that the growth rate of the world population in the period 1950-1973 was 1.92 % per annum, which roughly meant a population doubling every 35 years. This period was the so-called period of "population explosion" at a world scale since there had never before been such a high global population growth.

Entering into details, it is remarkable that in the "golden age" the annual population growth rate peaked in Latin America (2.73%), followed by Africa (2.33%) and Asia (ex-Japan) (2.19%). In the same period demographic behaviour of Europe land-marked a trough (0.70%), while the population in Japan grew at 1.15%, USSR and satellites evolved at 1.31%, and EIC group (US, Canada, Australia and New Zealand) grew at an average rate of 1.55%.

The average population growth rate of the world lost momentum in the "neo-liberal" age, moving from 1.92% to 1.66%. Most of the regions reduced their population growth rate with the dramatic exception of Africa, that reached an average figure of 2.73% per

---

73. Note that this extraordinary growth rate in Asia (ex-Japan) during the neo-liberal period should be mainly attributed to the 7 countries of fast growth rate, the so-called tigers (Hong Kong, Singapore, South Korea and Taiwan), and Malaysia, Thailand, and Mainland China.

annum, a rate capable of doubling the demography of the continent every 25 years. Latin America reduced its annual population growth rate at around 2%, a little bit over the growth rate of Asia (ex-Japan). Europe halved its previous growth from 0.70% to 0.32%, while USSR and satellites experienced the sharpest fall of the population growth rate from 1.31% to 0.51%.

Chart 2

Population, GDP, and per capita GDP 1950-1998
(average annual growth rate)

	GDP (%real terms)		Population		Per capita GDP	
	1950 -73	1973 -98	1950 -73	1973 -98	1950 -73	1973 -98
Western Europe	4.81	2.11	0.70	0.32	4.08	1.78
EIC group*	4.03	2.98	1.55	1.02	2.44	1.94
Japan	9.29	2.97	1.15	0.61	8.05	2.32
Asia(ex Japan)**	5.18	5.46	2.19	1.86	2.92	3.54
Latin America	5.33	3.02	2.73	2.01	2.52	0.99
Sov. Union& Satell.	4.84	-0.56	1.31	0.54	3.49	-1,10
Africa	4.45	2.74	2.33	2.73	2.07	0.01
World	4.91	3.01	1.92	1.66	2.93	1.33

Source: Maddison, A. (2001:126). The World Economy. A Millennium Perspective. OECD. The European Immigration Countries(EIC)*, include US, Canada, Australia and New Zealand; the group Asia (ex-Japan)** include 7 countries of fast growth rate (China, Hong-Kong, Malaysia, Singapore, South Korea, Taiwan and Thailand) plus 8 additional Asian countries with significant growth rate (Bangladesh, Burma, India, Indonesia, Nepal, Pakistan, Philippines and Sri Lanka).

A simple look at these figures enables us to identify *prima facie* the most problematic regions in the world. During the neo-liberal age, the case of the population growth rate in Africa, the poorest region of the world in terms of development and welfare, has been tragic in itself because it increased at a time when the golden age was over. This rate supposes *ceteris paribus* an enormous hindrance for the per capita income increase, forcing African governments to devote disproportionate budgetary efforts, just to maintain the already scant per capita level of their public goods supplies (health, education, infrastructure).

In this regard it would be convenient to remember that the population of Western Europe, as an average, never surpassed the figure of 0.77%, not even in the period of the "baby boom" (1950-1973). A figure that enabled greater internal savings (private and public) to finance its development process in the last two centuries. The sharp fall in the population growth rate in Russia is also a cause of concern limiting the possibilities for its catching up in terms of GDP.

3.1.3. *The per capita GDP growth in the world*

As a consequence of the annual evolution of the global GDP and the population per annum in the two mentioned periods of the last half of the 20th Century, the global per capita GDP also grew at different rates. In the golden age this per capita growth rate per annum was 2.9%, while in the neo-liberal era the former rate more than halved, reaching a figure of 1.33%.

In the golden age period, 1950-1973, the annual growth rate of the per capita GDP of Japan was the highest (8.05%) in the world, according to Chart 2. Even in this period of maximum prosperity, the per capita GDP of the African continent grew at the lowest rhythm (2.07%). The EIC group and Latin America registered a per capita GDP growth rate of around 2.5% per annum, while the per capita GDP in USSR and satellites grew at 3.49%. In this period the citizens of Western Europe experienced a significant increase in the per capita growth rate (4.08%) per annum, almost doubling the rates of the EIC group[74].

In the neo-liberal era the rhythm of prosperity experienced a generalised down fall[75] except in the case of Asia (ex-Japan). This region moved from an annual per capita GDP growth rate of 2.92% in the golden age, to a 3.54% in the neo-liberal period. In Eastern

---

74. The enormous effort of European citizens for reconstruction of war-torn Europe, initially facilitated by the Marshall Plan, made this per capita GDP growth rate possible. Japan experienced a similar development. Both profited from the economic battle of the US against communism in the early years of the cold war. Main European countries also profited from getting rid of independence wars in former colonies.

75. Among other things, the sharp increase of the price of energy, and the appearance of internal environment legislation in Western countries, forced a reduction of the former growth rate of productivity of labour.

Europe, on the contrary, this period was a clear catastrophe, not only in terms of economic performance, which significantly reduced the standard of living of their citizens (per capita GDP growth rate of – 1.10%) but also in its political functioning. Note that in the middle of the period the communist political and economic model of the region became bankrupt, and this was followed by a period of greater economic instability.

Chart 3

Evolution of the real p.c. GDP in prominent stages of capitalism (Weighted average of annual growth rates in different periods)

	1870-1913 Classical Liberalism	1950-73 Golden Age	1973-98 New Liberalism
Western Europe	1.32	4.08	1.78
EIC group	1.81	2.44	1.94
Japan	1.48	8.05	2.34
Total advanced countries	1.56	3.72	1.98
Asia (ex Japan)	0.38	2.92	3.54
Total Advanced plus Asia (ex Japan)	1.36	2.93	2.91
Other 40 count. of Asia	0.48	4.09	0.59
44 Latin Amerc. count.	1.79	2.52	0.99
Sov. Union & Satell. (27 countries)	1.15	3.49	-1.10
57 African countries	0.64	2.07	0.01
Total 168 shaking count.	1.16	2.94	-0.21
World	1.30	2.93	1.33

Source: Maddison, A. (2001: 129), book already mentioned.

Note: According to the specialists, the history of capitalism has evolved along 5 more or less agreed stages. Three of these stages are described in the Chart. We should also count with the period 1820-70 in which the annual p.c. growth rate of the World was 0.53%, and with the period 1913-50 in which the global growth rate was 0.91%.

The per capita GDP of Africa did not grow at all in the neo-liberal era (0.01% per annum), while Latin America grew only at a rhythm of 0.99%. Note that the lost of steam in Western Europe was also significant, experiencing an annual growth rate of per capita GDP (1.78%) which only surpassed Latin America, Africa and Eastern Europe.

3.2. Evolution of interregional differences of per capita GDP

As mentioned above the neo-classical model with its flexibility in prices of goods and services, and free mobility of all factors, will in the long run automatically[76] tend to equalise the per capita GDP of the different countries and regions. Any initial significant difference in the prices of factors, wages and interest rates, will in time become smaller, thus generating a trend of convergence in the standard of living of all citizens.

However it is clear that some natural barriers to trade and movements of factors do exist. One of these barriers refers to the so-called transactional costs. In this case, the larger the invested resources in settling contracts are, as happens for instance in the current process of international labour mobility, the lesser will be the profits stemming from interchange. As a consequence, an increase in the facilitation of contracting will favour the mobility of goods, services and factors, with gains for all players.

Another natural barrier to trade is the existence of significant transport and communication costs. These costs, defined as the value of economic resources necessary to move the commodities or information from one place to another, induce a limitation in the working of the principle of comparative advantage, mainly affecting those countries that are far from the world trade gravity centre.

Consequently the cheaper and quicker are the modes of communication and transport[77], the more perceivable will be the comparative advantage of the different countries, which ultimately would increase the gains of trade (if at the same time governments do not erect artificial barriers, tariffs and non tariff, to trade). Summing up, although these barriers to trade and movement of factors do exist, it is clear that the transactional, transport and communication costs per unit have in a monotonous way shown a

---

76. In the neo-classical model the word "automatic" does not involve any temporal reference to markets clearing. As a consequence the foreseeable process of convergence, implicit in this model, has no specific timeframe.

77. Costs of transports dramatically fall in the 19th century when railways and steamboats appeared on the horizon. In the 20th Century the development of transport by road, and the introduction of containers, have also reduced the costs of transport in a relevant way.

temporary decrease, thus making the functioning of the neo-classical corollaries in the international field easier.

Chart 4

Per capita GDP and inter-regional differences, 1870-1998 (in US dollars of 1990, PPP)

	1870	1913	1950	1973	1998
Western Europe	1974	3473	4594	11534	17921
Western Europe	1974	3473	4594	11534	17921
EIC group	2431	5257	9288	16172	26146
Japan	737	1387	1926	1439	20413
Asia (ex Japan)	543	640	635	1231	2936
Latin America	698	1511	2554	4531	5795
Sov.Union& Satell.	919	1501	2601	5729	4354
Africa	444	585	852	1365	1368
World	867	1510	2114	4104	5709
Disparity	5:1	9:1	15:1	13:1	19:1

Source: Maddison, A. (2001: 126), book already mentioned.

However, as measured by Maddison, the real convergence, (Chart 4) with the exception of the golden age period, did not move according to the expected outcomes of the neo-classical model. Firstly, in the period 1870-1913, also called the age of the "classical liberalism", the disparity of the per capita GDP among the different regions of the world, far from reducing, almost doubled, widening the gap between the most prosperous group of countries (EIC group) to the poorest one (Africa). This disparity became even greater between 1913 and 1950, which increased three-fold as compared to that of 1870.

Paradoxically in the golden age period (1950-1973), wherein public intervention in Western countries was more intense than before, and Keynesian policies were applied for reducing unemployment rates, the world economy experienced its quickest growth rate. At the same time the degree of regional disparities of per capita GDP downgraded from 15:1 to 13:1[78]. However in the neo-

---

78. It is also possible that the relative public expenditure in infrastructure and the setting up of public industries in developing countries experienced a hike, as a consequence of gaining their independence followed, by the implementation of import-substitution policies.

liberal era (1973-1998) also called "the age of globalisation", the disparity of per capita GDP of the different regions has mounted to the figure of 19:1.

As a consequence, the naked reality observed in the age of globalisation (in the neo-liberal era) is that despite expectations of convergence of the per capita GDP of the different regions by means of progressive liberalisation this has not become a reality[79]. Of course this does not mean that we should get rid of the current economic model, or look for more direct public intervention as practised in the past. However, in order to correct the problems of the current approach, we should get rid of its dysfunction and inefficiencies while introducing a more rational approach of the neo-classical model with a political priority for catching up and sustainability in a reasonable time-span.

3.3 People under poverty line as a paltry target

Note that in front of this growing per capita income gap, which is one of the main causes of discontent in the poorest countries today, the multilateral economic institutions and the Western countries have established a short-sighted target for its correction. In this regard, the velocity of reducing the absolute number of people below the so-called poverty line[80] has become a matter of discussion (speed of convergence, and role of ODA and FDI in this convergence), being this apparently the main target to be achieved.

This paltry target, veiling the main underlying problems that provoke mounting discontent (growing gap and exclusion) may in

---

79. There are other studies as for instance that of Prof. Sala-i-Martin of the Columbia University in New York, that suggests that the rising of incomes, especially in Asia, has created a "huge" middle class, thus making global incomes more equal. However, although according to this study the peak of the income distribution graph has moved slightly to the right, there is a segment of the population of the world and of every country that has remain deprived. At the same time in every country, and in the world, the income of the rich has augmented much more than that of the middle class. "Liberty's great advance", in The Economist, June 28th 2003 Special 160th Anniversary Issue.

80. This poverty line, defined as the minimum income to survive, figured out at one dollar per person a day, is used as an indicator for the effort to be made. Specifically the multilateral economic institutions have adopted the millennium target of halving the number of people under the poverty line (currently around 800 million people) by 2015. Note that this dollar-a-day poverty line has for more than a decade remained fixed, ignoring the PPP and exchange rates movements of the US dollar in this period.

the short-term, only be useful for sedating Western governments and citizens. In the new historical tempo, wherein basic human rights have been upgraded everywhere, this meagre target accompanied by others (primary education for all and improving health by 2015), even if they are fulfilled, cannot solve the enormous social problem faced by the world. Probably, the fulfilment of these targets will only worsen the social situation since the poor citizens of the poorest countries will become more aware of their relative deprivation, which may provoke more frustration and irritation. Note that in this regard the degree of discontent is a positive function of the awareness of relative differences in standards of living, and not of the progress of the non-ambitious absolute targets, as established by the millennium summit in September 2000.

3.4. Special consideration of the Muslim world

In the above lines we have suggested that poverty, extreme inequality within a society, and growing gaps between societies may be causes for conflict and extremist behaviour[81]. If we add to these conflicts growing political radicalism and religious fundamentalism, both motivated by long-standing political exclusion[82], the panorama for the worst is complete.

Looking at the Muslim world, mainly in North Africa and Asia, we have to say that most of these countries have a per capita GDP (in PPP terms) under the average of the per capita GDP of the world, which is well under the per capita GDP of the West. Among the Muslim countries, 10 communities have a per capita GDP even below 50 percent of the average GDP of the world.

If we now take into consideration the Muslim countries that have entered into conflicts (Chart 5), or could potentially enter into

---

81. A report by the World Bank published in May 2003 based on a study of 52 civil wars since 1960, reveals that contrary to public opinion, ethnic tensions and ancient political feuds are rarely the primary cause of civil war. Instead economic forces such as entrenched poverty and heavy dependence on exports of natural resources are usually to blame. Collier, Paul and others, World Bank, Washington DC.

82. One should not underestimate the frustration among citizens of these countries towards some ruling oligarchies, which are protected by Western leadership. This frustration is further strengthened by the Palestine issue, in which according to the Muslim world, under the argument of "religious historical" rights of Jews on territory, a significant Palestine population has been displaced.

conflicts with the West, it is clear that all of them are below the average per capita GDP of the world. Even more, all of them, except Iran and Algeria, and perhaps Libya, are well under the 50 percent of the world average. And some of them are even worse, with per capita GDP (in PPP terms) very far below the mentioned 50%.

Chart 5

Muslim World in conflict:
Evolution of the disparity of their per capita GDP

	1950	1973	1998	Per capita GDP (1998) PPP
Algeria	5.2	5.9	8,2	2688
Lybia	(..)	(..)	(..)	(..)
Sudan	6.7	11.8	24.9	883
Iran	4.1	2.5	5.2	4265
Iraq	5.2	3.7	19.5	1131
Yemen	7.3	7.9	9.6	2298
Bangladesh	13.2	27.8	27.1	813
Pakistan	11.1	14.5	11.4	1395
Afganistan	11.0	20.3	42.8	514

Source: Data from Maddison (2001) Annex A, book already mentioned and own elaboration.

Note: The figures of the Chart represent the quotient of the p.c. GDP of OECD countries, over the p.c. GDP of the mentioned Muslim countries.

In this regard one should admit that to accept disparities, in comparison with OECD countries, of almost 43 times in terms of per capita GDP-PPP, as in the case of Afghanistan in 1998, and to expect no frustrations and reactions against this very unfair situation, is simply not understandable. If someone in the international community had taken significant action long before to avoid reaching such a state, the episode of the twin towers perhaps might not have taken place.

Nevertheless, Afghanistan is not the only example that could generate, or that has generated, problems to the rest of the world. There are other countries, with a disparity of 27:1, in which some radical groups of citizens could pose problems to the international community in the near future. In any case countries with such extreme economic disparities are prone to trigger violent conflicts, a situation that should urgently be corrected by the international community using peaceful economic measures (increasing financing for development and facilitating trade)[83].

3.5. Trade, movements of capital, and convergence in 1950-1998

The above mentioned acceleration of the growth rate at a world scale in the period 1950-1998, was mainly due to the reconstruction (up to the 60s) of the war-torn countries in Europe and Japan, and the increase of public investments (up to the 70s) in the newly independent countries. It was also founded on the registered advances in the productivity of labour due to new technology and human effort. As a complement, mutual trade relations among the different regions of the world experienced a sharp increase, giving a further thrust to the process.

For instance, the growth rate of trade in raw materials surpassed that of the GDP. As an average the quotient between exports and GDP at a world scale moved from 5.5% in 1950 to 17.2% in 1998. Founded in new technologies, transport and communications also experienced an accelerated development, which allowed cheaper transports and faster spread of knowledge and information concerning other markets, thus increasing the opportunities for interchange.

The international flows of capital also increased very quickly. Although the great bulk of these flows were concentrated in the developed world, capital also flowed to developing countries of Asia, Latin America and Africa. As a consequence the gross value of accumulated foreign capital in developing countries, increased from 4% of their GDP in 1950 to 21.7% in 1998.

Note that this growing interchange has been promoted by some institutional developments. In particular the successive international

---

83. In the context of the low and middle income countries as a whole—following the jargon of the WB—the sole region of the world whose exports have grown below the world average in the decade 1991-2001 has been Middle-East and North Africa (the core of the Muslim World). Its exports of goods grew at an annual rate of 4.7% while the global exports of the world grew at 5.8% and the exports of the rest of the low and middle income regions grew well over the world average. World Bank (2003: 315) "03 World Development Indicators".

negotiations inside GATT have enabled the reduction of tariff and non-tariff barriers to trade, which has encouraged international trade. On the other hand the progressive liberalisation of international movements of capital has triggered the process of de-segmentation of former narrow financial markets of the nations, thus improving the efficiency of the international capital transactions.

However, the flows of private funds from the developed world to that of the developing ones, have mainly been directed towards a limited group of countries, namely those endowed with enough economic assets (strategic raw materials, infrastructure, educated population) to generate non risky and short term capital gains.

Some other developing countries received public foreign capitals (ODA) for political reasons, in order to strengthen barriers between the communist world and the West (South Korea etc). The developing countries that were not selected for any of the former reasons were mainly left to their own domestic possibilities to finance their development, which meant leaving their growth rates far from those of catching up.

China has been the most successful and most remarkable developing country in initiating convergence; a country that has since 1978 started a fast process of reform and development with investments mainly financed through domestic savings[84]. Although this country additionally receives around 4-5% of its GDP[85] through external savings, the bulk of this foreign financial effort is carried out by the Chinese community abroad (from Taiwan, Hong Kong, Singapore, South Korea, Indonesia, US, etc.).

3.6. An economic rupture: rising US versus declining EU

Till now we have mainly focused on comparing economic performances of the different regions of the planet, and we have expressed our concern about the sharp and growing per capita income disparities, as these combined with exclusion may unleash violent conflicts and also give rise to terrorism. This is the reason

---

84. It is convenient to remember that in 2000 the domestic savings rate of China in terms of GDP was around 40%.

85. It is important to emphasise the fact that 70% of FDI received by China comes from Hong Kong, Taiwan and other Chinese communities in neighbouring countries. This means that this seemingly foreign capital is also Chinese.

why, for the near future, we propose much larger and reorganised public transfers to LDC, and better access to markets in the West in order to promote economic convergence in a reasonable period of time.

We also believe that these transfers should be implemented multilaterally under the aegis of the UN, and that the correlation of economic and political powers within relevant UN institutions should change into a more balanced one. In opposition to certain ideas that normally come from those who enjoy the monopoly of power[86], the new power structure would also require constructive countervailing powers to take actions in order to reduce the contemporary dominance of the US on multilateral institutions. We do believe that a greater balance of power will serve the interest of all communities, including that of the American society.

Since the world cannot wait and should not wait for consolidation of other emerging countervailing powers (f.i. China and India)[87], the only available alternative in this decade is the construction of a countervailing power within the EU. At this moment, however, the political clout of EU in international issues is marginal, and even lesser than that of some of its individual members. Moreover, common sense suggests that neither Britain nor France can on their own, effectively counteract the dominance of the US, letting aside the experience that Britain seems to prefer joining the hegemonic power rather than counterbalancing it.

In addition, a real increase of political influence of the enlarged EU in international issues is not expectable. This is deducible from the recent role played by the EU in the Iraq issue, and from the fact that at this moment the political reorganisation of the EU (prepared by the Convention) is mainly geared at finding workable procedures for decision making after enlargement. The impossibility of reaching a common European stand in the case of unilateral military action

---

86. For instance the Foreign Secretary of UK, in an interview broadcast by the BBC on the 27th April 2003, suggested that in a uni-polar world it is unnecessary to establish any countervailing power, like France seemed to organise. This is an unexpected comment coming from someone who should believe in the advantages of cross controls in a global democratic system.

87. As forecasted by Goldman Sachs for the 2050 Horizon. Goldman Sachs (2003). Global Economic Papers. No 99. The authors of the report are Wilson, D. and Purushothaman, R.

against Iraq has perfectly proved the problem of non-homogeneity of the (future) collective of 25 countries.

This combined with the economic under performance of the EU-15 in the last two decades clarifies the need for an urgent and more in-depth political reorganisation of the EU. As we have proposed in another essay[88], this should be realised by means of a voluntary federation of some EU-12 member countries, willing to transfer some vital powers (defence, finance, security, foreign affairs) to a European Federal Government. Note that although this implies an EU at different speeds, already in the 90s the then EU subscribed to the idea of a European integration of different velocities. The existence of the current EU-12, with its members joining the monetary union and 3 EU countries remaining out, is a good example of that.

3.6.1. Evolution of the EU and the US in comparison to other economies

We have already depicted the different growth rates of the GDP and the per capita GDP of the Western European countries, in comparison to the EIC group (US, Canada, Australia and New Zealand). However, because of its relevance, we will now especially consider the case of the US, the current hegemonic power, in relation to GDP developments of the European Union.

The EU, known for its lack of political capabilities in international issues, also has significant deficiencies in its internal economic organisation, given the inflexibility of some of its relevant markets, and the exasperating gradualism in the process of decision making concerning common issues.

In order to evaluate the current economic potentiality of EU-15, it is relevant to compare the aggregated GDP figures of the EU countries with the corresponding figures of other relevant economic blocs or nations[89]. To have a first insight in the

---

88. Rahman, RD. and Andreu, JM. (2002b: 94). A Federation with Enlargement for European Prosperity. Rashtriya Printers. New Delhi.

89. These comparisons are typical in the official economic literature of the EU. While doing these comparisons however, one should not forget that the EU is not a country, but several countries until the moment of its political integration. This means that the EU GDP figures as a whole represent more a capacity of consumption and import of goods and services, than that of a joint economic action capacity, be these internal or external, and private or public.

economic relevance of the EU in a global context, we may refer to the figures of Chart 6. In this Chart we can see the importance of the aggregated GDP of the EU-15, which in 2000 was rather similar to that of the US or to that of the group of countries of the East Pacific basin (Japan, China and NIC). If instead of looking at the absolute value of GDP we consider the average per capita GDP (which is the relevant parameter to measure the degree of development and trade potentialities), we have to conclude that the US is heading the world, followed by (declining) Japan, and thereafter the EU.

Chart 6

Economic situation of EU-15 and other economic blocks
(GPD in PPP terms) 2000

	GDP (% of total)	Population World=100	Per Capita GDP Index (Average=100)
EU- 15	20.0	6.2	320
EU- 15	20.0	6.2	320
EU-11	16.0	5.0	321
US	22.0	4.6	478
Japan	7.3	2.1	348
China	11.6	21.1	55
Nics Asia	3.4	1.3	262
Russian Fed.	2.5	2.5	100
Latin America	8.4	8.5	99
India	4.6	16.6	28
Africa	3.2	12.2	26

Source: Economic Portrait of the European Union in 2001. Eurostat. EC (2001: 52)

In order to know the future economic potentialities of these countries, knowledge of their recent economic evolution is also relevant. An economic path, that when projected into the future may roughly describe the relative situation of these blocs and nations over a period ahead.

As we can see in Chart 7, the GDP of the US has evolved in the last two decades at an average annual rate of 3.2%. This figure is clearly higher than that of different members of the EU[90]. The growth rate of the US has also been larger than that of Japan (2.7%) in the last 20 years, although the latter has grown faster than the EU. The case of China is extraordinary with an average annual growth rate of 10.4% in these two decades, which signifies that *ceteris paribus*, this country could in next decades become a real economic super power.

Chart 7

Comparative evolution of the GDP 1980-1999

	1980-1990 (%)	1990-1999 (%)	Simple Average (%)	Per Capita GDP (US$ 1999) in terms of PPP
US	3.0	3.4	3.2	30.600
Japan	4.0	1.4	2.7	24.041
China	10.1	10.7	10.4	3.291
Europe (EU- 15)				
Austria	2.2	2.0	2.1	23.808
Belgium	1.9	1.7	1.8	24.200
Denmark	2.3	2.8	2.5	24.280
Finland	3.3	2.5	2.9	21.209
France	2.3	1.7	2.0	21.897
Germany	2.2	1.5	1.8	22.404
Greece	1.6	1.9	1.7	14.595
Ireland	3.2	7.9	5.5	19.180
Italy	2.4	1.2	1.8	20.751
Netherlands	2.3	2.7	2.5	23.052
Portugal	3.1	2.5	2.8	15.147
Spain	3.0	2.2	2.6	16.730
Sweden	2.3	1.5	1.9	20.824
U K	3.2	2.2	2.7	20.283

Source: World Development Report 2000-2001. Table 1. World Bank 2001.

Although it is clear that history never reproduces itself in all its details, since underlying parameters are never constant, the future position of different blocs, based on the *ceteris paribus* clause, could help in taking better informed decisions. The results of this exercise,

---

90. The economic growth of Ireland is an exception to the general rule, although this country is of little significance in our exercise, given its small population.

using GDP figures of the World Bank[91] for 1999, enable us to deduce several important traits of the world economy in 2015:

1. The GDP gap between the US and the EU-15 will increase in the following years reaching a figure of around 20% in the year 2015;

2. The GDP of China could in 15 years reach a size that could be around 70% higher than the GDP of Germany, and similar to the size of the German and France economies altogether;

3. In 2015 the GDP of Japan and China altogether will be as important as that of the EU-15; and

4. The economies of several EU-15 countries such as France, Germany, and Italy will significantly lose importance, moving towards a second tier position at global level[92].

3.6.2. Causes of the economic decline of EU-15

Note, that in the period 1980-1999, the European Union had lost steam in the global economic evolution, despite three processes of enlargement and two outstanding movements towards deepening integration among member countries[93]. The most elemental explanation for this decline is usually based on the deficient organisation of relevant EU markets.

It is a fact that the internal EU markets are much more segmented and less flexible as compared to the internal markets of the US. This is because the EU-15 governments have not sufficiently liberalised some markets (as agriculture and labour markets), while showing individual protectionist behaviour to the need of timely de-segmentation of others (as for instance convenient freedom in intra-European take-overs). Even more, they do not interchange sensitive

---

91. World Bank Development Report 2000-2001. With these figures we elaborated the commented projections in our common work A Federation with Enlargement for European Prosperity (2002:59), book already mentioned.

92. This idea regarding the loss of importance of main countries of the EU at the 2015 horizon, is also supported by the previously mentioned study of Goldman Sachs.

93. In this period, EU was enlarged with Greece (1981), Spain and Portugal (1986), and Austria, Sweden and Finland (1995). In the context of the EU, the European Single Act (1986) and the Treaty of the European Union (1992) were also signed.

information in relation to external markets, nor do they practise fair play among each other in international bidding. Additionally they officially protect their own national interest against agreed upon targets[94].

The result of the former considerations is clear. If EU as a whole or some crucial member countries do not progress towards political integration from the current under-performing-unstable Monetary Union, they will for long be in a situation of under-competitiveness and inefficiency concerning internal markets. If we add to this the lack of unity of action of the EU in relation to some external markets, we have to conclude that against this background, even with the same technological level, the GDP gap between the US and the EU will necessarily tend to increase.

From the point of view of aggregate supply, we could mention two additional causes for the different rates of economic growth registered by nations: 1) the evolution of the employed labour force of every country, which depends on the evolution of the country's population, its rates of activity, and its unemployment rates; and 2) the evolution of the productivity of the employed labour force, which depends on the rate of investment over the GDP, and on the evolution of the annual number of worked hours per worker.

Delving into the details, we observe that the majority of the EU countries (9 members) have in the last 20 years experienced average productivity growth rates, which were 25% less than that of the US[95]. The cases of France and Germany are alarming. These countries, being two of the largest economies in the EU, only obtained figures of 1.4% and 1.3% respectively, well under that of the US (2%).

Concerning the evolution of the investment rate[96], we observe that the annual average rate of domestic investments in the last two

---

94. The case of France officially rejecting due accommodation to public financial prescriptions of the Stability and Growth Pact is paradigmatic. The recent "freezing" of this Pact as decided in the Ecofin Meeting on 26 November 2003, may appear to have driven the EU-12 to a blind ally.

95. The sole EU country that has maintained a good pattern in relation to the evolution of its labour productivity in the last 20 years has been the UK. This country has even surpassed (2.2%) the figure of the US (2.0%).

96. The level of GDP per worker (its productivity) depends crucially on the level of available capital per worker. Vide Neoclassical Model of Economic Growth in Andreu, J.M. (1997: 360). Una Introduccion a la Macroeconomia. Dykinson. Madrid.

decades has been higher in the EU-15 than in the US, while the productivity per worker has increased at a slower rate than that of the US. This paradox can be explained in a very simple way: the decline of annual working hours per worker in the EU has more than compensated for the increase of productivity per hour in Europe as a consequence of greater investments[97]. Note that the new investments embody the newest technologies.

Finally, we will look into the evolution of the labour force, which is the other variable that explains the evolution of the GDP and the widening gap. In this regard we find that the growth rate of labour force, a proxy variable in the long term of the growth rate of the employed labour force, is clearly larger in the US than in the EU-15, with some exceptions (Ireland, Netherlands and Spain).

To conclude, the widening gap of the GDP observed in the last 20 years between US and EU-15 is due to the following causes: 1) the employed labour force has grown more in the US than in EU-15, pushed by a larger growth rate of its population; 2) the productivity of the labour force has grown faster in the US than in the EU-15, as a consequence of a higher preference for leisure by Europeans, despite a greater effort done by the EU countries in their gross domestic investment; and 3) the existence in the EU of badly organised internal markets (agriculture), the segmentation of others, particularly the labour markets, and the lack of competence and high concentration in many activities in the industrial and services sectors.

3.6.3. Corrections to enhance economic and political capabilities of the EU

In order to urgently establish a constructive countervailing power to the US in international matters, as well as to correct the increased GDP gap US-EU, observed in the "neo-liberal period", we

---

97. While between 1973 and 1998 the number of per capita working hours in Western Europe decreased 12.2%, that of the US increased 12.9%. The difference of these figures between the US and the EU for the considered 25 years represents an average growth rate of around 1% more hours per person, worked every year. Maddison, A. (2001: 132), book already mentioned. For similar considerations, Robert Gordon "Two Centuries of Economic Growth: Europe Chasing the American Frontier". Quoted in "The Economist", (2003:74) February 8th.

reiterate our earlier suggestion for construction of a Federation for Europe[98]. This Federation, that in our view could only be established on a voluntary basis among interested members of the current EU-12, could render relevant services to the international community in issues of conflict resolution, be these preventive or palliative.

These international preventive actions should be focussed on stepping up development co-operation for bridging the economic gap, which in our view is the most relevant cause of current insecurity. At the same time, the Federation could enable the European economy not only to catch up with the US, but also to boost their development co-operation budget.

The economic advantages of the construction of a (voluntary) European Federation are huge. Under the assumption that this Federation would for instance be established among 8 current EU-12 countries[99], this would amount to 60% of the current GDP of the EU-15. The GDP of this Federation would then be well over the GDP of Japan and more than three times the GDP of the UK, which would mean a significant change of the current economic power structure of the planet.

The construction of the above proposed Federation would generate at mid-long term relevant gains due to "economies of integration" that, as we have explored in another essay[100], could annually reach the figure of 2% of the GDP of the federated countries. To be specific, in the case of defence the voluntary European Federation could save 1% of its GDP. The former example is not but one, although perhaps the most important, in which the federation will gain economies of scale.

Note that the economies of integration that would be reached through the constitution of a federation (2% of its GDP) could be devoted to different activities, be these internal or external, without additional fiscal efforts of the taxpayers. The construction of a European Federation would also enable to overcome crossed public

---

98. Rahman, RD. and Andreu, JM. (2002b: 71), book already mentioned.

99. We have assumed as a working hypothesis, that this federation would include France, Germany, Belgium, Netherlands, Luxembourg, Portugal, Spain and Austria.

100. Rahman, RD. and Andreu, JM. (2002b: 70), book already mentioned.

deficit problems and inefficiencies in the implementation of the economic policy by the Union, thus reducing the risks of future economic downturns. Problems, which are basically, caused by the lack of instruments of the European Union and its partner countries, in their fight against cyclical economic dips[101].

Logically, the simplest manner for the correction of this anomaly, far from mildly reshuffling the existing bodies for co-operation or co-ordination, as outlined in the draft EU Constitution, would be the implementation of a Federation with full economic powers to develop an appropriate common micro and macroeconomic policy.

Summing up, the urgent promotion of a voluntary European Federation would help to significantly improve global governance and to rebalance the current international political situation that could be qualified as biased towards conservatism and degraded multilateralism.

3.7. The international economic institutions and the growing gap

Any overview of recent economic evolution in different regions of the world should include a closer look into the role played by the international economic institutions (International Monetary Fund, the World Bank and the World Trade Organisation). These institutions are not only charged with the task of preventing global depressions, but in addition they have become key-players in defining globalisation policies and in streamlining conditions for economic and trade progress.

The initiative to establish the IMF and the World Bank in 1944 had a twofold background. First, to stimulate the economic recovery and to avoid the disturbances generated by non-co-operative and globally inefficient practises during the global depression of the

---

101. This lack of capabilities would be irrelevant if the EU economies behave according to the postulates of the neo-classical model. A model that always drives the economies to a situation of full employment, on the assumption of total flexibility of prices of goods, services and factors. Unfortunately this assumption is not realistic in the EU either. For more details on the challenges of the European Monetary Union, Krugman, P. and Obstfeld, M. (2000: 634) International Economics, Theory and Policy, 5th Edition. Pearson Education Asia

30s[102]. And secondly, to rebuild the huge destruction of infrastructure and other physical assets provoked by the Second World War.

The initially designated roles for these two institutions were quite different and complementary. The IMF was devised mainly to give stability to the currencies of participating states, through a system of fixed exchange rates, based on the assumed long-term stability of the dollar. At the same time the IMF had to solve juncture problems of the signing countries, concerning their balances of payments. In those days, it was thought that a stable exchange rate framework would be conducive to increase international trade and to facilitate movements of capital with gains for all players.

The role of the World Bank on the other hand, was to finance the reconstruction and development of its founding members, primarily through the reconstruction of national infrastructures. In addition, an international accord to encourage the liberalisation of trade between the countries, the so-called General Agreement on Tariffs and Trade (GATT) was reached in 1948. In 1995 the GATT was incorporated into the ex novo established World Trade Organisation (WTO).

Although in the beginning the Bretton Woods institutions were mainly supporting the economies of the Western countries, the focus gradually shifted towards the economies of developing countries. Today, the ability to attract public foreign capital by developing countries is almost entirely determined by judgements on the status of their economies made by the IMF and the World Bank. Note also that this shift in targets and the multiplication of the number of members in the last decades has occurred without a significant change in the decision-making procedures of these institutions.

3.7.1. The role of the International Monetary Fund

The economic and political structure of the International Monetary Fund is similar to that of the World Bank. These two institutions are jointly owned by around 150 member-countries, but

---

102. In particular, we should here remember the war of exchange rates and tariffs put into practise by different western countries, in order to transfer their own high rates of unemployment to others, in times of the Great Depression. This action was later baptised as "begging the neighbour" policy. The policy of everyone trying to solve its own problems without seeking co-operation with the others, created a general reduction of international trade and a deepening in the industrial crisis.

the voting power of the members depends on the level of their annual contribution, which is proportional to the size of their economies. This mechanism tends to perpetuate its initial structure of power, favouring the influence of the main founding members in defining economic policies and recommendations.

As to the IMF, the Bretton Woods conference in 1944 established a system of fixed exchange rates against the US dollar. Till 1973, the year of the crumbling of this fixed exchange rate system, it was the responsibility of the IMF to finance temporary external deficits of the member countries, which did not require devaluation. However, when a country experienced a "fundamental imbalance" in its external economic position, it was authorised by IMF to devaluate its currency. At the same time, the latter, by supplying conditional funds for the implementation of stabilising policies, played the role of international lender of last resort, thus averting financial crises and avoiding its spreading.

Note that in the long term this system of fixed exchange rates (35 dollars per ounce-gold and fixed rates for the rest of the currencies against the dollar) could not work. This was due to the fact that gold, being at the core of the monetary system, was also a commodity, the market price of which depended on different circumstances of private transactions. For instance its flow of production, its demand for industrial purposes, and last but not the least speculation. Already in the 60s the non-feasibility of the system became patent and some governments started to officially exchange their accumulated dollars for gold[103], thus progressively eroding the gold reserves of the US, and consequently the confidence in the convertibility of the dollar.

As a precaution, already in the late 60s, the IMF created the so-called Special Drawing Rights (SDR), a sort of fiat money, whose creation was not dependent on the will of a sole country. This fiat money was in principle created to add liquidity to the system, given the fact that the volume of gold and dollars kept by different Central Banks grew insufficiently in relation to the volume of trade, which could potentially hinder commerce. Unfortunately these SDR never

---

103. We could remember that France was one of the first rushers for the American gold, thus forcing, with others, the reduction of the ratio between the American gold and the dollars circulating abroad. A manoeuvre that was caused by the lack of confidence in the dollar convertibility, thus further eroding that confidence.

played the expected role in the supply of international liquidity. This was mainly due to the lack of agreement on its distribution among different member countries. Consequently the dollar persisted being the core currency in international transactions, thus giving the US the opportunity to continue raising the so-called *seigniority rights*[104].

Following the breakdown of the previous system, a new one was born in the 70s: the floating exchange rates. By definition this new system did not require the use of significant funds from the IMF to support industrialised countries with problems when they had external deficits, because in that case they could freely opt for depreciation of their currencies.

In the wake of the two oil crises that drove many LDC to the ropes, the IMF necessarily had to change its role. The IMF now started to devote its efforts mainly to finance the balance of payments *disequilibria* of developing countries, by supplying them concessional (at low interest) loans. Observe that up to 1973 the conditions of these loans included keeping fixed exchange rates as a commitment. However, after the crumbling in 1973, conditions for granting loans veered to the practise of strict economic policies, the so-called IMF conditionality[105]. The use of this conditionality and the progressive participation of IMF in solving problems of developing countries resulted in an stretched involvement of IMF in the device of binding policies[106] for the economic growth of these countries.

---

104. The seignority right is a concept that stems from the age in which absolute monarchs coined metal and put the coins into circulation with a nominal value higher than the intrinsic one (as a commodity) of the metal contained in the coins. Because the current dollar banknotes have an almost nil cost of production, while their nominal is much higher than the cost, the difference between the nominal of notes and the cost of their production is the profit of putting dollars into circulation. As calculated, the nominal volume of notes outside the US, which are credit titles that never are presented to the debtor, generates for the US a seigniority right of around 0.1% of its GDP. Incidentally a figure equivalent to the ODA supplied by this country.

105. According to an IMF historian, "the use of resources was no longer undertaken in defence of a par value system, but to promote effective and durable adjustment and restoration of the conditions for balanced and sustained economic growth". Garritsen de Vries, M. (1986) The IMF in a Changing World, 1945-85. Washington DC. IMF

106. Normally the IMF played its role through the organisation of "financial packages" to solve critical situations in which, at times, developing countries were involved. These financial packages were (and are) usually agreements among IMF, the debtor country, and the crediting commercial banks. The agreements normally contained a compulsory package of macroeconomic measures to be adopted by the indebted country, which in exchange received fresh money from IMF and the commercial banks involved.

After the second oil crisis, in 1982, the external debt of the non-oil-exporting developing countries reached the figure of 600 billion US dollars, the half of which had been borrowed from multinational private banks[107]. The service of this huge external debt became extremely difficult to pay because of the contemporary high interest rates for its refinancing, and the appreciation of the US dollar. In order to avert a widespread default of private lenders, the IMF played a leading role in restructuring and refinancing the outstanding debt of developing countries. In the 90s the IMF also played a significant role in the Asian crisis (1997) motivated by a generalised flight of short-term capital out of some Eastern Asian countries, when the weakness of their banking systems became patent.

The role of the IMF and its policies in the Asian crisis has been strongly criticised by Stiglitz[108], who has accused the IMF of forcing developing countries to practise a "beggar-thyself" policy[109], consisting of the reduction of their GDP to cut imports and rebalance their current accounts. Note that these induced import reductions were exports of other countries. Consequently far from solving it, the mentioned IMF recipe induced a regional crisis.

In general the macroeconomic conditions imposed by IMF for debt refinancing were often conducive to severe reductions of the GDP growth of the indebted developing countries, consequently increasing poverty and enabling the enlargement of the gap. This is one of the main critiques on the debt-crisis-solving method of the IMF. A method that could be significantly changed in the context of our proposal for future boosted, pooled and reorganised international public transfers, given the fact that with this proposal LDC would gain certainty concerning future inflows of fresh money.

---

107. After the first oil crisis, the enormous external US dollar surpluses gathered by OPEC countries were mainly placed in international commercial banks. These banks undertook a parallel strategy of recycling these so-called petro-dollars by lending them to non-oil-producing developing countries, mainly in Latin America. When from 1980 onwards a new economic policy was put into practise by the Reagan administration, an escalation of interest rates occurred, producing a global recession that trapped developing countries. Their exports collapsed because of insufficient international demand, and the cost of servicing their debts shot up, thus placing the system in a situation of risk of widespread default.

108. Stiglitz, J. (2002: 106,107), book already mentioned.

109. This "beggar-thyself" policy has the same negative global effects as the "beggar-thy-neighbour" policy freely practised by European countries in the great depression of the 30s.

3.7.2. *The role of the World Bank*

While the IMF devoted its efforts to solve financial problems of balance of payments, the World Bank and its affiliates were initially involved in the internal reconstruction of war-torn Europe. When the reconstruction of Europe was finalised, the World Bank directed its attention mainly to investments in developing countries. Note that the loans granted by the International Bank for Reconstruction and Development (IBRD) were (and are) normally offered on commercial terms to governments or agencies of developing countries, or to public firms that have obtained government guarantees. The International Development Association (IDA) is the branch of the World Bank that provides additional support to the poorest countries, offering them credits on concessional terms, with longer repayment periods and softer interest rates. These two institutions (IBRD and IDA) form the core of the World Bank.

In the first two decades of its existence, the loans of the World Bank were basically directed to finance projects related to energy and transport in Europe, because it was understood that this type of investments, with its positive spill-over effects, would enhance quicker growth. From 70s onwards, this approach was transplanted to developing countries in order to step up their growth processes. Afterwards it appeared that this transplanted approach, mainly focussing on infrastructure and energy, could not be successful since in most developing countries industrial development was not only hindered by the lack of infrastructure, but also by the shortage of skilled labour and an inefficient institutional framework. This highlighted the so-called problem of absorption capacity in poor countries.

The World Bank loans were thereafter mainly directed to finance the agriculture sector, in particular cash crops for export, a strategy that was meant to contribute to the fight against poverty and to guarantee food security. Later on, when human capital development gained more attention, funds were also supplied to finance projects in the field of education, water supply and sanitation, and health care.

Additionally the World Bank offered other services such as technical support, economic research, provision of information and statistics, and so on. It should be underlined that since the late 70s, the World Bank also provides funds and technical assistance for "structural adjustment"[110] of LDC economies with permanent trade and public deficits.

Again, as it occurred with the IMF, in trying to reorganise the economic environment according to its version of the neo-classical model, the adjustment programmes devised by the World Bank were accused of not contributing to bridge the gap but, on the contrary, to increase inequality.

3.7.3. Policy convergence of IMF and World Bank

At the beginning, the IMF had the responsibility for the correction of external account disequilibria, forcing macroeconomic adjustments in exchange for loans to address foreign currency gaps. Alongside, the World Bank tried to increase domestic production of member states through microeconomic policies, mainly via project financing.

In the last three decades however, fast changes in the global economy (two oil-crisis, external debt crisis, significant and volatile movements of short-term capital, etc) have triggered a certain policy convergence of these two institutions.

For instance, to improve the external economic position of LDC vis-a-vis the developed world, the IMF not only recommends stabilisation policies to align the internal rate of inflation with the external ones. It also suggests corrections of internal markets for increasing efficiency, setting up fiscal reforms, and correction of exchange rate regimes. Note that some of these recommendations of the IMF overlapped with the traditional areas of assistance of the World Bank.

Conversely the World Bank, upgrading its activities, started looking into the external factors that limited the success of its microeconomic programmes in LDC, thus introducing recommendations for enhancing international competitiveness in these countries through the reform of their trade and exchange rate policies.

---

110. These structural adjustment programmes, usually exacted in exchange for granting loans, later on evolved into the so-called "Washington Consensus" conditions.

It is clear that the promotion of stability of external accounts cannot guarantee growth and prosperity. At the same time the promotion of growth could be conducive to structural deficits of LDC. Therefore it was necessary that both institutions entered into the competencies of the other, in search of own consistency and co-ordination. No wonder that their political recommendations finally coincided in what we have depicted as the Washington Consensus. We reiterate here that in our view, the conditions considered as "necessary" by the Washington Consensus are neither necessary nor sufficient for catching up.

Given the fact that the role played by IMF will continue being necessary, the only suggestion we have for its future is that the IMF should continue devoting its efforts to secure global financial stability, but at the same time it should deploy greater accountability and intellectual independence. Its statute should also change, bringing in a new political structure in line with the changes we will recommend for the UN. Conversely, since in our view the way to encourage development should significantly change in profile and magnitude, we propose that all World Bank institutions should be reorganised and incorporated in one global organisation for development financing, under the aegis of the UN. This approach will be worked out in Chapter 6.

3.7.4. *The role of the World Trade Organisation*

In 1947, around 25 countries, mostly developed ones signed the so-called General Agreement on Tariffs and Trade (GATT). Along the following years a number of newcomers adhered to the Agreement, and after the crumbling of the USSR, most countries of the world have become party to it.

After the Uruguay Round in 1995, the World Trade Organisation (WTO) was established and the GATT became one of its basic legal pillars. The other pillars were the General Agreement on Trade and Services (GATS) and the Agreement on Trade Related Aspects of Intellectual Property Rights (TRIPS). At this moment the 145 members of the WTO account for well over 90 % of the world trade, and virtually all the FDI. Note that one of the main principles of the WTO is that all its members are tied to all obligations (GATT, GATS, TRIPS and any other agreements).

The initial aim of GATT was to liberalise international trade. This has been achieved along successive negotiations among participants via reduction of custom tariffs and progressive elimination of other barriers to trade. Of the 8 celebrated negotiations, the so-called Trade Rounds[111], the first 5 which took place between 1947 and 1961, focussed only on reduction of tariffs, while the number of countries involved was very small (between 13 and 38).

This limited activity was due to the fact that in this period most developing countries had embraced "import substitution" policies, to encourage internal industrial growth and development, thus lacking interest in negotiations on the reduction of external tariffs. In the Kennedy Round (1964-1967) the number of participants grew considerably and antidumping measures were also analysed. In the Tokyo Round, which finished at the end of the 70s, non-tariff barriers were also considered. Finally in the Uruguay Round a decision was taken to establish the WTO, and new issues were introduced for further negotiations: services, intellectual property, textiles, agriculture and so on.

Along these negotiations, often very painstaking, the involved blocs of countries have been prone to maintain double standard. They have tried to figure out the exact level of protectionism of other countries that always have been qualified as high, while justifying their own protectionism by "very relevant" economic arguments. These arguments were based on protection of the nascent industries, fight against the dumping of the others, preservation of the domestic employment, existence of negative externalities in the production of certain goods outside the country, etc. Some times they have also provided other non-economic reasons (related to self-sufficiency and non-dependence, preservation of their own style of life, etc.) that normally imply high opportunity costs.

The negotiations have basically progressed in a general framework that followed some fixed rules: 1) the so-called "clause of

---

111. These rounds took place in: Geneva 1947, Annecy 1949, Torquay 1951, Genoa 1956, Geneva 1961 (Dillon Round), Geneva 1967 (Kennedy Round), Geneva 1979 (Tokyo Round), and Geneva 1988 (Uruguay Round).

most favoured nation"[112]; 2) the general prohibition of establishing new quantitative restrictions or quotas; 3) the special and more favourable treatment granted to LDC (Generalised Special Preferences); and 4) the general prohibition of retaliation measures against the exports of others.

Nevertheless after the difficult times that followed the two-oil crisis, many countries resumed certain protectionist practices. These were implemented by means of the introduction of non-tariff barriers, such as establishing implicit subsidies to domestic productions; prohibition of certain imports on the wake of safeguarding sanitary or food security rules according to domestic standards; intentional delays in customs procedures; etc. All these letting aside the low quotas related to access of agriculture products maintained by developed countries, in particular EU and US. In the Uruguay Round these new ways of protectionism were protractedly discussed, resulting in the establishment of WTO, a settled multilateral organisation to deal with international trade and trade related issues.

3.7.4.1. On the trade policies to be put into practice up to 2005

Until 1995 the non tariff barriers imposed by rich countries, such as hard-small quotas in their agricultural imports (theoretically equivalent to high tariff rates), sanitary regulations, multiplicity of standards, etc, were the most meaningful obstacles for the export capacities of LDC. On the other hand, we have to mention that, in the process of dismantling their tariff barriers, the rich countries kept exceptions in the form of peak tariffs[113] mainly for processed food products exported by developing countries, thus creating an additional difficulty for the industrialisation of these countries. At the same time these protective measures of the rich

---

112. This clause forces any country that has made a special tariff concession to others, to extend them to the rest of the partners of GATT. One main exception to this clause is the possibility that a group of countries could sign a regional free trade agreement, without extending the agreed mutual preferences to the rest of GATT participants.

113. The game of tariff peaks established by some Western countries implies that market access for more processed products (embodying greater value added) is more restrictive. For example, in EU and Japan fully processed food products face tariffs twice as large as products in the first stage of processing. In Canada the ratio is even higher: 12 times higher than for non-processed products. For more details Stern, N. (2002: 12), book already mentioned.

countries have averted the necessary accumulation of foreign reserves by developing countries, for which the latter often have been criticised by the IMF.

The WTO, created in the Uruguay Round, was meant to supervise further trade agreements and settle trade disputes. Concerning the interests of developing countries three major provisions were agreed upon:

1) Developed countries were to cut tariffs on manufactures by 40% phasing cuts over 5 years. Additionally industrial tariffs of rich countries were eliminated in 10 export sectors, which however were almost all irrelevant for developing countries. In exchange developing countries agreed not to increase tariffs and to proceed with trade reforms;

2) Trade on agriculture products came under the authority of the WTO and would progressively be liberalised, meaning that non tariff barriers of rich countries had to be changed into tariffs, although over a long span of time. At the same time agriculture subsidies would also be reduced, although slowly; and

3) For textiles and garments, 2005 would phase out the quotas related to the Multi-Fiber Agreement, which hindered the exports of developing countries. However tariffs on textile imports experienced an insignificant reduction.

Concerning the outcome of the Uruguay Round, we have to say that the implementation of the agreed issues has been, and still is, a constant matter of complains by developing countries. On top of that, in the so-called ministerial meetings scheduled every two years[114], new issues have appeared. The most remarkable ones have been the so-called Singapore issues (investment and trade, competition policy, transparency in government procurement, and trade facilitation) which are considered by developing countries to be mainly in the interest of the rich countries.

---

114. These ministerial meetings took place in Singapore 1996, Geneva 1998, Seattle 1999, Doha 2001, and Cancun 2003. The ministerial meetings have been established to monitor and review progress in implementation of Uruguay Round, and to promote new initiatives for enhancing trade. Some of these meetings, particularly those of Seattle and Cancun ended with noisy failures.

3.7.4.2. On the evaluation of GATT and WTO

It is indisputable that along the years the role of GATT has been positive in enhancing trade, by stimulating the lowering of tariff barriers in successive rounds of trade negotiations. We have to underline however, that global trade has also been enhanced by other relevant economic variables, in particular the increase of GDP of different countries, and the relative reduction of distances in terms of costs of transport, which dramatically fell.

Leaving aside the relative merits of WTO negotiations in fostering international trade[115], one should recognise that, in the successive processes of bargaining, the different power positions of the players have generated asymmetrical results in favour of the rich world[116]. The methodology of negotiations on the basis of consensus has basically followed a *quid pro quo* attitude, far from historical responsibilities of the richer parties, thus contributing to the growing economic gap, as we have mentioned in the lines above.

The well-established fact that the share of exports of developing countries has more or less kept its quota in the last 30 years at around 25% of the total world exports[117] proves that the rich countries, although boasting about their leadership in liberalisation, have maintained rather conservative positions. Particularly in the dismantling of some barriers, such as those of agriculture and services, while increasing other non-tariff barriers. Even worse, although the global relation of trade to GDP has risen in the considered period, this ratio has almost halved for the least developed 44 poor countries.

---

115. Note that an important country as China has not only increased the volume of its international trade, but also has dramatically gained share in total international exports and imports, while not being a member of WTO. The success of the international trade of China cannot solely be attributed to the spill-over effects created by the WTO framework, but to other variables such as the cheapness of its industrial workers, productivity rise, the exchange rate of the yuan and to the specific traits of its administration.

116. The fact that the export share of the low and middle income countries has remained around ¼ of the global exports in the last 30 years, does not signifies neutral behaviour of the West, but rather manners consistent with the observed growing economic gap.

117. Todaro, M. (2000: 461). Economic Development. 7th Edition. Addison-Wesley. Vide also Maddison, A. (2001: 360), book already mentioned and World Bank (2003: 314) "03 World Development Indicators".

To complete the profile of exports from developing countries, we could mention that the share of exports from developing countries going to other developing countries has increased dramatically from the 60s onwards, from around 17% to nearly 40%[118]. The former figures of exports shares of developing countries (global share fluctuating at around 25% and South-South share at 40%) imply that in the neo-liberal age the export quota of these countries to the West has significantly declined[119]. This is in sharp contrast to what was aimed at with the Generalised Special Preferences granted to LDC inside the GATT. On the other hand this means that the general trend in international trade has been in favour of increasing regional trade[120], not promoting trade globalisation, the main target of WTO[121]. However, this may be a "second best" solution for the developing countries, mainly caused by the relative in-accessibility of the markets of the West[122].

One should also note that with the new issues of WTO, the so-called Singapore and sustainability issues, the rich countries are putting more pressure on competition, labour social issues,

---

118. This increase in South-South exports is partly due to recent established regional free-trade areas such as ASEAN and MERCOSUR. The trend also reflects the development successes of LDC in Asia, whose economies have been growing faster than in Western countries. Unfortunately, once again Africa has been left out of the game. Todaro, M. and Smith, S. (2003: 547) Economic Development, 8th Edition Pearson Education

119. Of course this has not always been the case. According to the figures provided by WB for the period 1991-200, the low and middle income countries have significantly gained quota in the total global exports. Vide WB (2003: 315). Report already mentioned.

120. Note in this regard that while the intra trade in the EU has hugely increased in the last two decades, the extra-EU imports have significantly decreased in comparison to the total world imports. The share of the EU global imports has fallen from 24% of the total in 1980 to 18.9% in 2002. This seems to indicate that the commercial process in the EU in the past 20 years has generated a significant "trade diversion" effect with severe negative impact on the interests of developing countries and on the image of the EU as an alleged freer market defender.

121. As we have mentioned before this increase of intra-trade in developing countries has been especially visible in the period 1991-2001. This new trend only failed in the region Middle East and North of Africa, whose intra-trade grew well below the world exports average.

122. A proof of the unwillingness to improve western market accessibility can be found in the recent "castling" trade manoeuvre of the US and EU for perpetual agriculture protectionism devised one month before Cancun. According to Ernesto Zedillo, former president of Mexico, this unexpected US-EU alliance was the fundamental cause of the Doha round debacle at Cancun. Forbes, August 13 2003, quoted in Development News, 4 November 2003. World Bank.

environment matters etc., forgetting their own development history. We agree that some of these social and environmental failures in developing countries should be corrected as soon as possible. Nonetheless to use these issues as a pretext to hamper exports from developing countries, is not only asymmetric in its logic[123] but also very unfair in historical terms. To tackle these problems the rich countries should increase public transfers to these developing countries, in order to promote their development, thus correcting as a derivative these problems outside the international trade agenda.

In essence the purported good intentions of GATT and WTO negotiations have neither resulted in an appropriate growth rate of the multilateral trade, nor in the free movement of factors as the neo-classical model defends, in order to achieve the "promised-land" of economic convergence. And these improvements have not occurred because the approach to the neo-classical model defended by Western countries and Washington Consensus has been a selective one based on short term self interest, and managed in favour of the few and not the many. Note that although GATT/ WTO has a history of more transparency and less biased behaviour than the Bretton Woods institutions, its current agenda still mainly reflects the interest of its more affluent members.

---

123. It is remarkable that when developing countries have tried to add labour market liberalisation to the WTO agenda, they have been sent to the ILO (international labour organisation), while conversely the issue of child labour has prominently been put on the WTO agenda by the rich countries, as if this phenomenon has never existed in the rich world along the last century.

4

Evolution of Political Philosophy and Developments in the Political Framework

In the former chapters we have depicted the configuration of the current economic philosophy (chapter 2) and its global economic results (chapter 3), to some extent induced by doctrine and actions of the international economic institutions. In this chapter we will focus on the evolution of the political framework in which the different economic philosophies have developed, and on the outcomes of its implementation.

Note that the ideal construction of the first rational economic model (Smithian economics) practically coincided in time with the French revolution. This coincidence was not accidental. The freedom of the market, central in the Smithian economics, required a framework of political liberties. However, any change in the political framework has to confront vested interests and existing power structures. This is the reason why the march towards a larger freedom and more players in political and economic processes, took a lot of time. We should here remember that in Britain, the cradle-country of these ideas, it took around 70 years before this free-market approach seriously started to work.

In the French revolution the ideal of political freedom was defined along the ideals of equality and brotherhood, which nowadays may be revisited as equality of opportunities and effective solidarity. Along the last two centuries both ideals of economic and political freedom, conducive to efficient economic interchange and equal opportunities (or even utopian equity), have been in the core of political discussions, political reshaping of states, and even internal uprisings or inter-states armed conflicts.

Given the fact that market freedom and political liberty cannot be exercised without a minimum background of economic resources in the hands of individuals, some previous growth or redistribution of economic goods were necessary to overcome the stage of serfdom.

4.1. Current Darwinism and consumerism in the rich world

Since any progressive movement has its conservative counterpart as two extremes of a continuum, Darwinism appeared also in the theories of social life in opposition to the ideals of equality and brotherhood. As a consequence of a Darwinian concept of life, some philosophers in the first third of the 20th century considered solidarity as something detrimental to the speed of progression of the fittest.

Nowadays this Darwinian idea, transplanted to economics, is presented under the garb that solidarity usually results in economic disincentives for the poor. Of course this presentation is mainly in vogue in rich countries, wherein the achievement of solidarity by internal development of a welfare state is no longer an individual concern for the vast majority. No wonder that these citizens of rich countries focussed on their selves, neglects not only their faraway neighbours, the poor of the world, but also those nearby. These is clearly an irrational behaviour, given the fact that a stubborn and long-lasting neglect of the others is always conducive to negative spill-over effects in terms of security and mid and long term prosperity for all, as history has proved at a regional level.

At present, citizens of Western countries, brain-washed by media, have a short-term focus. This means that they not only neglect others, but also neglect themselves in the long term. This self-neglecting attitude has different manifestations. At the core of it is the lack of a clear understanding whether the primary objective of their existence is to enjoy community life and social interaction to fulfil their basic human needs, being work or savings mere tools. Or, if alternatively, the target is an endless race to consume more than others, sacrificing human socialisation and leisure[124].

It is remarkable that recent polls indicate that most of the US citizens are dissatisfied with the current distribution between working hours and leisure time. At the same time it is notorious that they

---

124. We should here reiterate that the amount of annual worked hours by Americans is well over those worked by Europeans.

have to invest more than others do in private security. A paradox in a rich society, which claims to be the pioneer of freedom, in which people are increasingly lesser free and more locked in.

On the other hand it is also noticeable that in the last decades the Western leaders are often less influenced by rationale than by opinion polls, which show them what they have to do to remain in power after next elections. This impedes their performance as responsible leaders, who should take decisions with a long-term perspective, thus contributing to the interests of their citizens in a global context. Conversely, before making decisions, they mainly consult polls, whose outputs are often mere snapshots of short-sighted and inward-looking communities, thus closing a vicious circle.

No wonder that the mood and current philosophy of life of the western citizens, which ignore cross-border poverty and exclusion, drive their politicians to a dangerous long-term inaction concerning main issues for the international community. And this, while politicians try to preserve the present style of life of their voters, be this in economic international negotiations or by mismanaging of violent conflicts appearing abroad.

4.2. Rethinking the trade-off between efficiency and equity

Today few people would defend dictatorship against democracy, since the latter is a superior political system of selecting alternative targets[125], leaders and representatives to govern their countries under the rule of law. However, one of the main shortcomings of current democracies is that often the leadership only stimulates the debate on short-term issues, without assessing the long-term consequences. No wonder that in the parliaments of current democracies, many a times some projects or political actions desirable from the point of view of equity or solidarity, are not implemented, are downsized, or are indefinitely postponed due to their alleged lack of efficiency or their de-stimulation effects.

---

125. Note that after the crumbling of the Soviet Union, the controversy on core issues concerning the engine of political and economic progress has practically disappeared in Western Countries. In their parliaments petty things related merely to the aerodynamics of the system are discussed. As a consequence, one can notice steady internal erosion in the democratic life (less people exerting their voting rights and degraded debate among party manifestos).

Nevertheless we have to argue here that in some cases, as history has proven, these apparent de-stimulation and negative effects on the efficiency of short-term equity actions, are more than offset by mid-long term advantages. These advantages normally stem from the significant improvement in the environment or climate in which the economy and business have to operate.

In this regard, one should not forget that in the conventional neo-classical economy, the production functions considered as something related exclusively to engineering or technical relations among factors of production, have also to include the "organisation" of them. An organisation that has to adjust to the dominant ideas about what is considered as desirable by the society in connection with industrial relations (working schedules, shifts, security, holidays, leaves of absences, geographical mobility, etc), thus imposing restrictions on the use of labour by firms. Although these restrictions are limitations of pure technical relations and free contracting, few people would support the abolishment of them.

On the other hand, one should also take into account possible disruptions of labour markets, generated by previous situations deemed unfair by trade unions. With exceptions, rather at mid than long term, the two involved sides (in negotiations) make adjustments with each other to reach fair solutions, which often are not far from those of the market equilibrium. Consequently, the ideas about what are fair industrial relations have exerted a very significant and positive effect on the concept of long-term productivity. A concept much more comprehensive than the cold short-term productivity of labour stemming from mere technical relations of factors, and sometimes from the abuse of workers.

Having said that, it is not difficult to transplant these microeconomic ideas to the global macro-economy, productivity performance, and global prosperity. Accordingly, what sometimes appears as an unproductive expenditure, is in the long term a profitable action for all sides[126]. The history of the construction of welfare states in Western countries and the disappearance of former

---

126. Elson, D. (1998) "The trade off between equity and efficiency". Comment to the report "Gender and Economic Development". Netherlands Economic Institute. In this comment it is clearly stated that "In general, all the policies that decrease social unrest also stimulate growth and efficiency".

dramatic conflicts in labour markets, is an indisputable proof of that. Concluding, long-term measures taken to reduce unacceptable differences in the living standards of citizens (via public expenditure in education and health), or setting up rules to ease industrial disputes, should be considered as positive, and not against the efficiency of the production system. As a result, there is a trade-off relation between efficiency and equality in short-term, but it is beyond any doubt that sufficient equity cannot be neglected in the long term to gain efficiency.

4.3. Freedom, efficiency, and equality in history

In the last two centuries the relative emphasis put by governments on freedom and equity has gradually changed for the better, although with some temporal step-backs. Initially, the most advanced countries progressed towards liberalisation by getting rid of former limitations in economic interchange, sponsored by "mercantilism"[127]. As liberalisation progressed and the economy grew, the former rural population began concentrating in urban areas[128], earning their living in dehumanising sweatshops. In the name of freedom of contracting, also applicable to labour markets, these negative practises were patronised by nascent liberal states. Although this structural change enabled a significant growth rate of GDP[129], it drove the new urban workers into economic living conditions often worse than those in the countryside.

---

127. Mercantilism was a doctrine that defended that all the economic measures taken by states should be exclusively directed to the enrichment of the states themselves, neglecting the wellbeing of citizens. In order to reach these targets industry and commerce were intervened by public sector and guilds. In particular, the game of economic international relationships was based on encouraging trade mainly to colonies, while the imports were highly restricted. This kind of policy allowed the states to increase their gold and silver reserves, useful to finance expansionary adventures in benefit of the then great states (France, Spain, UK,...) in conflict. This economic approach entered into crisis with the writings of new economic philosophers, such as Smith and Ricardo. These authors stressed the idea that the wealth of nations was based on the richness of their citizens (not of the states), thus encouraging free economic relations among citizens and companies.

128. The percentage of urban population in Western Europe in 1820 was 12.3%. In 1890 this figure increased up to 31.0%. Maddison, A. (2001: 40), book already mentioned.

129. The average growth rate of GDP experienced in Western Europe in the 19th century was around 1.5%, while the growth rate of the population was around 0.7%, thus facilitating a per capita GDP growth rate of around 0.8-0.9% in Europe. This last figure enabled more than doubling of the European per capita GDP in the 19th century. Note that the velocity of prosperity was higher in the so-called EIC group.

Note however that in the last decades of the 19th Century a countervailing power, unionism, came into being, enhanced by two main factors: the Marxist ideas and the feasibility of spreading them among the workers concentrated in industrialising cities. For long the liberal states were not very concerned with the evolution of distribution of income and living conditions of workers, thus making a choice for efficiency while neglecting many social aspects of economic life.

When labour unions started their protest-actions with strikes, sabotages and pickets, the liberal states sent the police or the army to mainly protect the freedom of contracting. For long the behaviour of the liberal states concerning fair wages and "human rights" of workers was one of non-consideration. Of course this was a fertile breeding ground for the appearance of new socialist and communist parties who campaigned for better living conditions, a more general franchising, and even revolution.

The former negative relations among the social agents patronised by liberal states could be considered similar to the current economic and political relations at global level, between the developed world and the poor countries. Note that some extremist groups in poor countries, in the name of fighting against poverty or exclusion, also sabotage the convenient life of Westerners, as did the unionists in Europe in the first decades of the 20th century. One may observe also that the current difference in military destruction capacity between the West and the LDC is enormous, although similar to the power difference between the army sent by liberal states against the workers and the power of their unions. Despite these differences in power, the workers in Europe finally reached a more fair distribution in the 20th century.

It seems to us that the long period of 50-60 years wasted by the western liberal states in addressing their internal social problems caused by the abuse of the working class, which stemmed as a by-product of a non-restricted freedom of contracting, should not be replicated at a global level. However, in the past 20 years the practise in international negotiations has tended to this replication. Reacting by only sending armies to states in which extremists are assumedly sheltered is just a short-term purported solution, and an unfortunate repetition of history. Conversely, the implementation of a complementary, boosted, pooled and reorganised financing for development and improving trade accessibility seems to us a more effective solution of the problem at mid and long term.

4.4. Violent conflicts and the birth of the United Nations

At the beginning of the 20th century the main political problems to be addressed by European countries were basically three. First, the aspiration of greater representation in parliaments by ordinary citizens, most of them discontent and poor in the absence of a significant middle class. And this in front of the constant hurdles put by the establishment who feared to open up, while extremists pushed for violent revolution. Second, the existence of absolute monarchs in Central and Eastern Europe, who did not want to give an inch of their effective power to parliaments, while the social situation in these countries was also worrying. And third, the existence of an untenable regional organisation of one of the empires, that did not give way to the aspirations of its diverse nationals.

Probably it was not so much the political assassination of a royal in 1914 that ignited the war, but a combination of several factors. Here we could mention the defective organisation of the Austrian Empire, the irrational policy of alliances between states just to balance military power and the disproportionate retaliation after the murder. Four years later, unexpectedly, two of these empires disappeared, and with them the three main absolute monarchies of Europe.

Soon after the peace treaties were signed, a new dangerous cocktail was again in the making: the unstable German Republic of Weimar; the revolution-exporting Soviet Union; and a mosaic of small states as heirs of the Austrian empire. Note that in the Far East, Japan also continued its political and geographical expansions in the region, and in Italy an aggressive reaction against the communist threat took power.

In Germany, the Great Depression, the frustrations over the results of the First World War, the irresponsible internal political alliances and the fear for communism, drove into power an unscrupulous extremist group, with a European geographical expansionary doctrine. After taking power democratically they choked the democratic system and started huge human rights violations, political aggressions and forced annexations. The outcome of the above mentioned facts are very well known: a war in which millions of people died in Europe and Asia with huge destruction of assets.

Some months before the end of the war, China, Soviet Union, France, UK and US, met in Dumbarton Oaks, US, to draft a Charter for the United Nations. In June 1945, the representatives of 50 nations signed this Charter. The United Nations officially started its activities in October 1945 when the Charter was fully ratified.

In the Preamble of this Charter the founding members expressed their determination to avert more wars, to reaffirm the dignity of people, their fundamental human rights, the equality of men and women, and of nations large and small... and to promote social progress and better standards of life in larger freedom. To fulfil these aims the Preamble encouraged the practise of tolerance, good neighbourly relations and to unite forces to keep international peace and security, while employing international machinery for the promotion of economic and social prosperity for all peoples. Unfortunately the following sixty years proved that the Preamble was mainly a document of good intentions.

The new Charter established six organs: 1) the General Assembly composed by representatives of all member-states, each of them having one vote; 2) the Security Council, primary responsible for keeping international peace and security, with 5 permanent members, and 10 rotating ones elected biennially by the General Assembly. Note that the decisions in the Security Council are taken with a minimum support of 9 out of the 15 members, but these 9 must include the 5 permanent members, thus giving them a veto right; 3) the Economic and Social Council, as the principal organ to co-ordinate economic and social work of the UN and specialised agencies; 4) A Trusteeship Council, initially established to provide international supervision over 11 territories, which ended its work in 1994; 5) An International Court of Justice to settle legal disputes between states and give advisory opinions to the general Assembly; and 6) the Secretariat working to carry out diverse jobs for the organisation. At its head is the Secretary General, appointed by the General Assembly.

4.5. Evolution of international power sharing 1945-2003

The representatives of the 50 countries who met in 1945 in Dumbarton Oaks, committed themselves to establish a global institution for international power sharing. The main aim was to prevent the global community from the devastating experience of war and destruction, as the European continent had experienced twice within a short period of 30 years.

4.5.1. De-colonisation and aid

Moreover, the end of the Second World War also marked the start of the de-colonisation process of quite a number of states in Asia and Africa, sometimes after violent liberation wars with the already weakened colonisers. As a consequence the need for power sharing and for development co-operation was broadly felt and clearly expressed in the Charter of the United Nations. Soon after, the newly independent states started putting claims for support. These claims were often formulated in terms of rights to compensation for destruction during their independence wars, or for debts due to exploitation during the colonial days. Although they requested that their programmes for reconstruction should be incorporated in those for Europe (Marshall Plan), external financial flows to former colonies remained scant and incidental.

In those days the World Bank was mainly involved in the reconstruction of Europe, devoting little attention to poor countries[130]. Once the European reconstruction was finalised, bilateral development aid to former colonies was introduced. Note that the emphasis was on "aid", as a gift, instead of compensation as it had been proposed by the newly independent states. However, although the donors themselves had experienced the positive effects of the

---

130. In the 50s and 60s all the economic development doctrine hinged on the industrialisation process of poor countries combined with the theory of the substitution of imports. The economic models based on "big push" (Rossenstein-Rodan and Nurkse), mixed with the industrialisation model of Arthur Lewis, were at the core of the different development plans. Arthur Lewis believed that the excessive agricultural labour force could be transferred without significant costs to urban industrial production, and for long without increasing wages. The results of these experiments, although positive, initially worsened the distribution of income, in line with the famous "Kuznets curve", thus increasing poverty in the suburbs of industrial cities. Logically, in poorest countries this reversal of distribution resulted politically untenable and the development policy had to change.

Marshall Plan as a financial transfer between equals, they now ignored the request for compensation and gave preference to a scant and one-sided conditioned approach.

In the beginning of the 60s, against the background of communist take over in China, North Korea and Cuba, the threat of communism became a strong playing card in the hands of the leadership of the newly independent states (in Africa, Asia) and in Latin America. In these vital days of the cold war, economic aid and military intervention were the two main instruments used in the rivalry game between the two blocs. Some pro-western countries, bordering these mentioned communist states gained from massive aid, in particular South Korea. In other countries, mainly in Latin America and Africa, the West often supported military dictatorships, as an alleged necessity to establish strong governments in weak states.

In these cold war days many lengthy debates on basic human rights, the right to development and its financing, and the right to self-determination, were on the agenda of the General Assembly of the United Nations. As a result, numerous commissions, *ad hoc* working groups and other advisory bodies were established, including more and more specialised agencies in reaction to an even greater jungle of policy studies, reports and recommendations. At the same time some crucial resolutions adopted by the Security Council were simply not implemented, often because the defiant countries could count with the support of one of the veto-right holders, be these the US or the Soviet Union.

Within some decades the United Nations has become the most comprehensive global institution, with some important successes since its birth, but also with many imperfections in terms of democratic decision making and in sanctioning the non-implementation of its resolutions. Great shortcomings in peacemaking and peacekeeping could also be recalled.

4.5.2 *The birth of the NATO*

Despite multilateral (good) intentions and the agreement on global treatment of conflicts, soon after the end of the Second World War, the full support of the Soviet Union to the communist revolution in Czechoslovakia triggered strong reactions in the West, resulting in the creation of the Western Union. NATO followed this in April 1949. Note that this treaty for mutual assistance and solidarity in case of external attacks was signed by the US, Canada, the five countries of the Western Union (France, UK, Belgium, Netherlands and Luxembourg) plus Portugal, Italy, Iceland, Denmark and Norway.

Since the Western countries considered that the Soviet Union had violated the rules for peaceful co-existence, they decided to create a collective defence system, mainly as a deterrent to avert territorial adventures of the Soviet Union within the NATO territory. In reaction the Soviet Union established the Warsaw Pact among the countries behind the iron curtain.

The appearance of these two military blocs also marked the birth of a relentless arms race, whose protagonists were basically the US and the USSR. Nevertheless UK and France soon embodied into the "selective" club of nuclear powers, more to keep their old prestige than to lead in the game.

As any specialist in logistics knows, a long-lasting war, be this cold or real, cannot be gained without a flourishing economy supporting it. Although it was not known for decades, the arms race and the financing of conflicts abroad progressively conditioned the economy of the Soviet Union. Logically, this huge but unbalanced economic effort in weaponry expenditure, and even in the space race[131], made by an inflexible economy without any individual stimuli, could not last. Not even in a world with segmented flows of information.

Against this background, the economic effort for keeping up the arms race became more and more unsustainable for the Soviet bloc. The non-sustainability became patent, as the USSR felt it could not follow the pace of the US in the so-called Stars war (introduced by Reagan), while the per capita consumption of Russians was kept subdued to support a non-winnable race.

Due to modern communication technology, Western information started spreading in the 80s through satellites, and the citizens of the

---

131. There was a moment, in the first days of the space race, in early 60s, that the Soviets seemed to be heading the Americans. Since this facet of the arms race was relevant, the Americans rushed and finally obtained decisive advantage in the days of the so-called "Star Wars". As the dice were cast, from this moment onwards the Soviet Union was forced to relinquish a race that it could not gain, given the sad condition of its economy.

East bloc became aware of the way of living of their neighbours as compared to theirs. In this context of progressive discontent generated by access to free information, the crumbling process of "real socialism" was a matter of time. If we add to the above arguments the war in Afghanistan, in which for the first time after the Second World War, the Soviet Union had to pay a big tally with losses in material and lives, the non-feasibility of the Soviet Union became clear, even for the Russians. Accordingly, in a few years time, the assumed alternative to the West in economic and political fields melted like a sugar cube in a cup of coffee.

During the cold war, the former mentioned countries (USSR, US, UK and France), were not the only big players in the world. One should not forget Continental China (People's Republic of China) which soon after the communist came into power, tried to replace the Republic of China (Taiwan) in the Security Council as the fifth permanent member. Just a decade after the birth of this new colossal red state, China started showcasing remarkable differences with the Soviet Union, trying to appear as a more leftist republic than its northern neighbour was. Episodes as the frontier tensions with Soviet Union, the war against India, and the so-called Cultural Revolution were issues of relevant magnitude for public opinion in Western countries. However, after a period of internal instability and fights for power, this enormous country changed its economic approach, starting its liberalisation process in 1978. A decade later, in the 90s, China emerged decidedly as an economic competitor of stagnant Japan.

4.5.3 Power sharing in the 80s and the appearance of a hegemonic power

In the middle of the 80s the political correlation of power was like this. There was a country, the US, which economically grew at a higher rate than most EU countries, thus enabling it to pursue with the cold war arms race without this being an unbearable burden for American citizens. The Soviet Union on the other hand, had politically entered into a comatose situation. The ruling ideology and praxis, as managed by an outdated gerontocracy, did not offer solutions for contemporary problems, the weapons race was lost, and the Soviet economy was bankrupt due to lack of stimuli and an unsupportable defence budget. On top of that, the trade unions of some allied states started protests, strikes and demonstrations against the owner of public factories: the state. This contradiction could not last and did not last.

In the middle of the chaos in the Soviet bloc, mainstream Germany initiated conversations for unification with the Democratic Republic of Germany. The Information technology had finally played its role, waking up among East-Germans the desire for democratisation and access to western consumer goods and lifestyle. Also China after two decades of political infighting and strong economic decline, suddenly changed its economic system into a more market oriented one.

In the 80s the EU was merely a pledge of a political union (after a decade of euro-sclerosis it had signed the Single Act to arrive at the third phase of integration, a common market). Years later, after reaching a Monetary Union, the EU continued with its comparatively small growth rates of GDP, while indulging in small growth rates of its population, which enabled the EU to achieve higher growth rates of per capita consumption. And with few exceptions, mainly Britain, the EU countries kept meaningfully smaller military expenditures in terms of GDP as compared to the US.

In this general context, the US became the main player and the rest could only think and speak, but not act significantly. Besides the traditional non-linear political behaviour of the US, based on a case by case approach, did not change. This non-systematic approach has undermined the UN, and driven the EU to a dramatic choice between two options. Either to adjust to the external policy of the US, with little to gain in the long term, since the current US policy is basically one-sided, non-multilateral and consequently clearly defective for improving world stability and human security; or to emerge as a credible autonomous countervailing power.

This constructive countervailing power could be based on putting in common parts of the current sovereignty of some European States to create a voluntary Federation[132]. This

---

132. The first draft of the European Constitution, published in May 2003, outlined in a veiled manner the possibility that a group of countries inside the European Union progress further by creating a deeper integration among them.

development could in the long term change the political weight of the US and the EU in the world, and facilitate the process towards a more democratic UN, without any additional cost for EU citizens, as we have suggested[133].

It is beyond any reasonable doubt that any hegemonic power in national or international politics, or in economics, tend to produce political abuse and monopolistic behaviour in the interest of few, and not in the interest of many. This is a temptation suffered by most of the monopolies, be these economic or political, given the propensity of human behaviour, to act selfishly.

Consequently, if we want to avoid inefficient economic decision making at a global level or a constant dominating behaviour by the current hegemonic power in international policy[134], it is absolutely necessary to create constructive countervailing powers. We do believe that this power sharing would be advantageous for all, as it basically happens in economics with the introduction of more competitors in a monopolistic market.

In brief, as we defend the idea of market liberalisation against monopolies in the interest of global consumers, we similarly defend a multi-polar distribution of political power in the interest of global communities. Although we acknowledge that the introduction of countervailing powers will not be easy, it should be a priority for all.

4.5.4 The NATO in the new context

As a consequence of the crumbling of the Soviet Union, and the disappearance of the Warsaw Pact, the NATO started undergoing mutations in its targets and in its composition. Candidate members for the EU enlargement successfully applied for NATO membership as well as some other former Soviet Union satellites.

---

133. Rahman, RD. and Andreu, JM. (2002b: 30), book already mentioned. An integrated Armed Forces, an integrated Foreign Service, an integrated Borders Police and so on, will allow the member-states that take part in the envisaged political union, budgetary savings up to 2% of their overall GDP.

134. This hegemonic power has defined, without consulting the rest, the countries that are in the "axis of evil", and has simultaneously protected other countries that violate, or do not fulfil, the Resolutions of the UN. In other cases, when "failed states" do not affect the relevant supplies of raw materials or its national security, the hegemonic power shows little interest. With exceptions to save its own image, the hegemonic power generally shows a certain apathy to alleviate poverty.

However just months after these NATO enlargement, and as a consequence of the Iraq war, a new division between members took shape: those members acting multilaterally under the aegis of the UN vis-a-vis those joining a small coalition of countries lead by the US and acting on own account. Theses development provoked a reconsideration of the future targets of the NATO and of the role within the NATO of an EU army. Note that this EU army that could appear in the near future as a result of the defence clause in the EU Constitution, would embody the armies of France, Germany, and other significant EU countries, which today still operate within a NATO led by US.

Logically, the eventual redistribution of the power play in this context is provoking a real political storm in NATO headquarters between those that want to keep the current NATO power structure untouched and those that opt for change. One only has to consider that an EU army, even only combining military force of the initial EU-6 countries, would have a staff of more than one million, which is four times the army of UK, and a military expenditure tripling that of the British army in absolute terms[135].

Although the total annual expenditure in defence of this hypothetical EU-6 army would currently be around the 40% of that of the US, and its personnel a 30% less, the formation of this EU army would significantly influence the formation of will in the NATO as well as target setting and organisation. No wonder that severe concerns have been expressed by the US.

---

135. These figures and references have been reckoned using the figures on "Defence Expenditures and trade in arms" provided by the World Bank (2003: 288). 03 World Development Indicators. As well as other indicators concerning the different GDP.

5

Lessons of the Past and
Implications for the Future

In Chapter 3 the economic evolution of the different countries, and the growing economic gap among nations has been described. In Chapter 4, it has been clarified that due to the on-line spread of information, the current economic gap can no longer be maintained without all sides involved taking huge risks in terms of increased instability and conflict. Against this backdrop, the Western countries amazingly continue to defend their previous myopic economic positions, concerning financing development of LDC and trade negotiations.

Accordingly, it seems that Western countries have neither taken historical precedents into consideration, nor drawn lessons from them. The scant attention for the promotion of welfare in developing countries could be interpreted as if the leadership of the world is nowadays fully satisfied with the economic results of the current approach of the neo-classical model. However we do believe that in the very context of this model there are other more efficient interpretations of how to organise the economic life (internally and internationally).

It is difficult to imagine the state of the world in 10 or 20 years time, if the uneven economic North-South relations continue as they have been in the last 30 years. Nevertheless we will attempt to outline some possible consequences based on historical evidence and current trends. In our opinion, if nothing significantly changes, the economic gap will increase continuously in parallel with more violent conflicts, significant decrease in human security, pervasive uncertainty and perhaps global stagnation. Nevertheless this situation could be prevented if rich countries, or at least a majority of them, act with more acumen.

5.1. From an unfair-stable to an unfair-unstable situation

If we observe the economic and political history of Europe, we may deduce that many of the negative events that occurred in the last years of the 19th Century and the first half of the 20th Century could have been averted without significant long term economic sacrifices by the rich. In particular, if the then economic and political powerful groups had acted with a rational long- term prospect.

Going back in history, one could remember the ancient world of the watertight agricultural labour markets, typical of the pre-industrialisation age. These were markets completely segmented, reason being that it was then possible that wages on the different markets were divers, and indefinitely placed in very low positions[136]. We will add that in this context, the entire surplus was for the landlords, the owners of the then sole scant factor: the land. Logically the different surpluses obtained by landlords had to do with the difference in quality of their plots[137].

In any case, this unfair social situation, typical of agriculture societies, could continue indefinitely because the different labour markets were not connected, there was no accessible information, and the egalitarian philosophies that so much would change the world, had not become popular. Consequently for centuries social injustice and political stability could co-exist, and co-existed.

5.1.1. Urban societies and Marxism

This unfair and not so "naturally" balanced world however, collapsed with the arrival of industrial-urban societies. In these

---

136. The theory of "subsistence wages", delivered among others by Smith, clearly reflected the idea that the labour market in the long term would always tend to generate subsistence wages. According to the ideas of Smith it would be possible that these wages grew for a while, but the incidence of this growth in the evolution of population (increasing it), would force future reductions of wages, thus making them to converge again to subsistence rates. Note that this theory was abandoned many decades later because it did not consider the growth rate of labour productivity and the evolution of modern demography (independent of economic fluctuations).

137. The theory of the land rent is original from David Ricardo. This classical author explained that if it were possible to freely find non-exploited land of acceptable quality, then no one would pay a rent for using others land. However, if this not be the case as most arable land was already exploited (as it happened in Britain at the beginning of 19th Century), everybody who wanted to take over a plot, would have to pay a rent to the owner. This rent would be variable according to the quality of the land. As a consequence, the competition between tenants, increasing rents paid, would deprive them of any surplus, which would instead only be enjoyed by the owners.

societies wages of every market were known by players, and the idea of exploitation of labour by the owners of the new scant factor (capital) started gaining ground. In this context, the second industrial revolution witnessed some of the direct results of the neo-classical model when non competitive behaviour is out of control, in particular in abusive labour markets, or simply when the outcome of free competence in labour markets generates famine wages. Styled facts that occurred in consistency with an unprecedented industrial growth rate in the Western European countries and North America[138].

In this unfair framework, a simple but non operative new theory (Marxism) easily gained ground, as it explained some causes of observed problems of income sharing, working conditions and economic fluctuations. Similarly trade unions gained ground in the struggle for better wages and labour conditions for workers.

In those days the Trade Unions acted primarily as a mechanism of information dissemination among their associates and used certain tools to support negotiations, such as strikes, pickets, and so on. In some cases, when the harassment by owners or police was extreme, desperate unionists even resorted to sabotage. In any case the development of unionism was not easy. It is to be noted that in the quasi-democratic western societies of those days, trade unionism appeared hand in hand with socialist parties. These parties tried to gain political clout to legally improve the conditions of workers.

The derivatives of the principle of action and reaction were many-fold in the political (sometimes-violent) battle for taking power, or simply in negotiations on working conditions. Based on the growing fear felt by industrial owners concerning consolidation of socialism, fascist, corporate movements, or other purported "third ways" appeared. In these movements the role of the state would be rightist, prominent and totalitarian. Since many of the socialist parties did not gain significant advancement in the cause of workers, other parties (communists) veered towards revolution in order to constitute proletarian dictatorships.

---

138. These facts are nowadays well observable, for instance in South Asia, where many people do all kinds of jobs they could make to earn a minimal living. It is interesting to visit these areas. Just opening their eyes there, extreme defenders of the current approach of the neo-classical model would reconsider previous intellectual positions (although not necessarily).

In the middle of these new and in some cases threatening political stances, the traditional leadership, prone to merely defend formal rights without paying significant attention to social aspects, remained unattractive to the masses in most of European countries. The result of the stubborn blindness of the rich (concerning the social rights of the majority), who were in control of key positions in the traditional societies, drove Europe to a social and political escalation with a tragic balance of two world wars. Let us insist here that if the European masses had not been deprived, these wars probably would not have become a reality.

5.1.2. *Emergence of a welfare state inside Europe: a non-exported model*

Fortunately, after two human and material catastrophes, the European governments learned a lesson of history and started building the so-called welfare state. The previous economic exploitation of the masses by firms, and the frequent human rights violations by the machinery of traditional-formal democracies, should no longer be a pattern of behaviour. The costs (two European wars and constant social unrest) generated by these political short-sighted exercises, were huge and could not continue after the Second World War.

With the establishment of the welfare state the social scene changed, but only inside Western Europe. The behaviour of this sub-continent in relation with the rest of the world continued being short-ranged although to a lesser extent than that of the US. For decades, the Western countries, including Europe, have not been capable of organising a decent financing plan to solve, in a reasonable period of time, the (catching up) economic problems of the developing countries, many of them former colonies. Clearly, this has been again a bad choice that progressively and subtly has entangled the Western countries in serious problems of human security, social unrest, and economic uncertainty.

5.2. Delayed win-win solution: the European welfare state

Soon after the Second World War, the different Western European countries started the construction of their welfare states. The creation of more sufficient and fairer fiscal systems, plus the unprecedented growth rate of the western economies in the "golden age" period (1950-1973), encouraged the different EU states to construct public systems of pensions, national health services, and public education at all levels, thus promoting equal opportunities for all.

Few of the rich who at the beginning of the 20th century opposed the construction of the welfare state, could have imagined that some decades later the huge costs of building the welfare state, would result in a highly profitable situation for the European societies. This huge economic effort done in the name of internal solidarity, despite some recent cuts to gain efficiency has proven its relevance in the long-term increase of productivity, by means of guaranteeing social stability and supplying of abundant human capital.

The new European democracies also introduced or consecrated the concept of the minimum wage. The establishing of this minimum wage, although criticised by many economists after the 70s, because it introduced an element of inflexibility that decreased the availability of jobs in some situations, for decades played an important social role in some Western European countries[139].

Inside Western countries, the new public financial possibilities of the "golden age" period also allowed the setting up of internal regional policies, mainly dealing with the creation of sufficient infrastructure to improve connections among markets of different regions. This new public search for correcting internal geographical imbalances, although it too had its enemies, also reaped significant good results in terms of economic homogenisation inside the countries. The same could be said in relation to the interregional transfers of funds organised by the European Union to facilitate the catching up of the poorest new comers.

It has been said that the setting up of these welfare state systems as they have been depicted lines above, brought inefficiencies, and this is true. Although the intentions of legislators were good, in many

---

139. When the minimum wages were established in Europe they were welcomed because in many cases the effectively paid wages were under their levels of competitive equilibrium, thus additionally generating less employment. This means that some former labour market situations were oligopolistic or, at least, non-competitive. With the introduction of the minimum wages in those days the average paid salaries rose and the level of employment increased.

cases the possibility of misusing public funds appeared. However, as in any "trial and error" procedure, the initially committed mistakes should not encourage the scrapping of the welfare systems but its progressive correction, thus making efficiency and equity co-exist to the maximum extent.

In this regard, the current observable trend in Europe to indiscriminately degrade the role of the public sector, pushed by some market fundamentalists, is something that should be carefully analysed, because it could jeopardise future social peace. To sacrifice social peace for encouraging short-term efficiency would be an absurdity conducive to commit mistakes in timing and aims thus sacrificing long term prosperity (in consistency with opportunities for all).

Chart 8

Total public expenditure in terms of
GDP in Western Europe, US, and Japan

	1913	1938	1950	1973	1999
France	8.9	23.2	27.6	38.8	52.4
Germany	17.7	42.4	30.4	42.0	47.6
Netherlands	8.2	21.7	26.8	45.5	43.8
U.K.	13.3	28.8	34.2	45.5	39.7
US	8.0	19.8	21.4	31.1	30.1
Japan	14.2	30.3	19.8	22.9	38.1

Source: Madison, A.(2001:135), book already mentioned.

5.2.1. *Public firms and EU integration*

Another mechanism that in the aftermath of the Second World War could have played a very important role in the promotion of social peace in Western European countries, was the creation of public firms (many of them transferred from the private sector). With our current point of view, we could say that many of these public firms became at one stage inefficient. This is true, but it is also true that this public production served in many cases the interest of making softer some processes of industrial restructuring (after bankruptcy of private firms).

On the other hand, many public firms were created to cover some strategic aims, or just to upgrade competence. It is clear that nowadays many of their industrial productions can no longer be conceptualised as strategic, and competence has been upgraded by means of increasing trade, in particular among the EU partners. This was a sufficient reason for downsizing the number and importance of public firms.

The process of European integration has also had a positive contribution in the economic field, as well as in the promotion of internal social peace. In particular it has brought the development of the infrastructure of transports and communications, as modern mechanisms for promoting interregional and international trade. This in the long term will tend to equalise the factor prices, although the intra-EU movement of some of these factors (labour) has not reached significant figures as yet.

5.3. Europe and its relation to LDC in the era of welfare state

Setting aside the US, which for decades continued getting its own way in its relations with LDC[140], Europe overlooking historical lessons learned in the first half of 20th Century also focused on itself, instead of making a sufficient effort for the promotion of growth in developing countries. In the 90s western selfishness even increased and progressed in the wrong direction. This has been a decade in which the spreading of a new US-lead international capitalism, combined with fragmented, insufficient and non organised development aid and inconvenient trade rules, have worsen the problem of the growing gap.

One should not forget that in the golden age (1950-1973) there was a significant difference in approach between Europe and US, concerning the economic promotion of developing countries. Later on, although with exceptions, the European economic policy towards developing countries became similar to that encouraged by the US and the Washington Consensus. In its latest version, the Washington

---

140. In this period the US was in absolute terms the leading donor (basically a geopolitical one), although very modest in terms of GDP. Perhaps this has happened because the US never believed in international public transfers as an effective mechanism for enhancing development.

Consensus policy deals with transplanting to LDC an economic model of international relations that, in our view, cannot work efficiently but after longer periods of transition, and conditioned to the setting up of enabling infrastructure.

Due to the fact that the mentioned economic approach is defective in the application of some crucial corollaries of neo-classicism[141], it would necessarily generate sub-optima outcomes. In this regard we believe that few academician-economists would agree on the possibility of reaching an optimum in global welfare, by means of encouraging a free and two-sided international flow of funds, whereas international flows of labour are almost forbidden.

From the perspective of the outsiders, one could wonder why relevant professional economists or academicians have not devoted more time to explain the problems contained in the Washington Consensus approach. The answer is quite clear and was explained almost 3 decades ago by Feyerabend, a famous methodologist of science[142]. Whoever goes against the mainstream runs the risk of becoming isolated not only in academic circles but also in obtaining research funding or political postings. Circumstances that many a times creates among scientists an invincible fear to exhibit discrepancies, particularly on relevant issues. Regrettably this fear uses to be during a period a drag for the progression of the knowledge and action.

5.4. Expectable reactions of LDC to the behaviour of the West

It is surprising to see how current Western governments, who should be well aware of the catastrophic results of exploitation of informed poor[143] as it happened in Europe before the Second World War, are repeating the same mistake regarding their relation with the

---

141. It is curious that some contemporary communists, who in other times defended political stances far from those stemming from the neo-classical model, have today started defending the international free movement of labour, as a more consistent approach for income distribution.

142. This author, in his famous contribution, denounced the fact that against believed, the way of advancing in science was not so linear, objective, and based on falsification of former theories, as proposed by Popper, but impregnated by limitative sociological components. Feyerabend, P.C. (1975). Against Method: An outline of an anarchistic theory of knowledge. New Left Books. London.

143. Of course there have been other cases in history but not simultaneously in the same Continent.

developing countries. If one takes into account the resumed international growing economic gap since the 70s, one becomes bewildered facing the indifference and lack of acumen shown by the current Western leadership.

Perhaps the distance in time and civilisation made this international neglect more understandable in the first decades of the second half of the 20th Century than in present days. Much more amazing has been the maintenance of this stance in the 80s and 90s. In particular when in the last decade the historical tempo has changed with the great leap forward in information technology and communications. It appears as if the rich are barely concerned with the fate of the rest of human beings in the world, believing that it could not effect their lives and communities. This is a clear misconception since the negative effects of the oblivion of the poor are already perceivable in terms of human security.

It is surprising that at this turning point in history, no relevant Western country or multilateral organisation has tried to project the current trends, and to suggest some measures to significantly correct[144] the traits of a *ceteris paribus* predictable non-brilliant future. Only some individuals have undertone the convenience of using different or complementary strategies, or real commitments for the promotion of development. Against general opinion, these approaches would not be expensive in terms of GDP, could improve the standards of life of many, and could save in mid-long term millions of human lives from wars, diseases, and environmental disasters.

5.4.1. *Way out of deprivation: the increase of illegal migration*

At times in western democratic countries we can hear that the easiest form of eliminating certain illegal activities is to liberalise them, while keeping them under state supervision. Note that the outcome of banning these activities, is the automatic appearance of illegal organisations, or *Mafiosi*, that try to take advantage of the existence of a highly unsatisfied demand of corresponding goods and services. Observe that these crooks do that, irrespective of whether

---

144. The most worked out proposal to correct the present economic and political problems of the world has been presented by the UN, with the so-called UN Millennium targets. However there is a clear consensus on the little scope and likely lack of success in accomplishing these Millennium Targets.

these activities are intrinsically perverse (because of their very negative spill-over effects) as it happens with drugs-trafficking, or not. An example of the latter (not intrinsically bad) activities is the right of people to earn a living by means of working abroad, although this activity has been declared illegal.

In our view, the current problems of growing illegal immigration in Western Countries or its lateral derivatives, as that of "bogus asylum seeking" (both having increased recently in intensity), are to great extent a consequence of the lack of sufficient co-operation of rich countries. This deficient co-operation has happened in particular in WTO issues and in development financing. The rich countries have kept their frontiers watertight to the reception of low-skilled foreign workers. And this, although neo-classical economists always emphasise that the public powers never have been successful in their battles against the law of demand and supply. This is an "invisible power" against which, neither the police nor the missiles of Western countries can result victorious in the long term, as one cannot fight against the law of gravity.

We have to add that the migration processes have never been easy, neither for migrants nor for host countries. In principle, migrants are often forced to move out from their countries by circumstances of poverty or lack of job opportunities. In this context, if Western countries were capable of implementing an adequate development financing in poor countries, and if the former ones would be less egoistic in WTO negotiations, many problems due to illegal migration could be avoided.

To conclude, illegal migration is a by-product of backwardness in the countries of origin of migrants, and of prohibitions of labour movements that affects ordinary people in need of work and search of a better world for their families. Consequently to legally impede the international movements of people, without taking complementary measures in the field of development financing or trade facilitation to LDC, is clearly a sterile manoeuvre for unsustainable protectionism that does not make sense.

5.4.2. Emergence of national and international terrorism

Longstanding sentiments of frustration, often derived from endless suffering due to sheer exclusion and abject poverty, are sometimes conducive to violent reactions. This phenomenon is well known by psychologists, who have studied this behaviour not only among poor or discriminated people in rich countries, but also among the excluded in poor countries. This aggressive reaction may generate internal terrorism or an external one. Normally internal terrorism, be this from separatist movements or due to promotion of political uprisings, do not produce general concern at international level, because their targets are always pursued within own boundaries.

A cause of more concern for the Westerners is the appearance in the 90s of international terrorism. This is simply a new type of guerrilla-war, organised and declared by international groups of terrorists, based or not in so-called "rogue states", against one or several formal states, mainly the hegemonic power and its allies. These terrorist groups act against citizens or economic interests of the countries declared as targets, seemingly at random, in any part of the world and at any time.

The emergence of this type of terrorism, with its spectacular and dramatic attacks, for example the "September 11", the "Bali blast" and the Istanbul case, is highly worrying and feared by targeted citizens. Note that this wide spread fear[145] among westerners is based on the alleged progressive easiness of making or acquiring weapons of mass destruction (WMD) by terrorists, or on the fragility of modern transport and infrastructure. The fear of these western citizens multiplied with the possibility that terrorists might use home made weapons to shoot down planes while landing or taking off[146].

The big question that arises these days, is whether the declared war against terrorism by the US and eventual colluded powers, will actually achieve the wiping out of international terrorism or will not. We do believe that while economic, cultural and technological gaps continue to grow, the ground for frustrations will increase along with its likely derivative of hatred and violence. On the other hand, to the extent that violence against terrorism is practised in a frontal way, as

---

145. This fear is to some extent irrational and over-in-reaction, taking into account the scant probability that such terrorist attacks affect many individuals at the same time.

146. As occurred in Mombassa, Kenya, against an "El Al" plane, or more recently in Bagdad against a courier-plane of DHL.

it has been the case until now, its results could be meagre against a so slippery and self-reproductive enemy.

Note additionally that when terror actions occur, they will always be based on "coups de main", seemly at random, with no space to defend, and never openly and not with publicity in advance. Consequently the prevention and reaction against this sort of actions should be a matter of intelligence instead of frontal attacks against isolated states that allegedly protect terrorists; and this in parallel to a much more visible and effective collaboration in development and commercial issues by Western countries. We do believe that in this case no LDC government would protect international terrorism.

5.4.3. *Potential reactions of developing countries if bridging the gap fails*

In the lines above we have depicted some natural reactions (migration) of LDC citizens in order to individually escape the nasty effects of the growing gap. Afterwards we have mentioned the possibility of the formation of international groups of terrorists; groups that simply try to implement noisy and spectacular revenges against targeted rich western citizens and their governments.

Nevertheless in the lines below, we will detach from the previously described practises carried out by individuals or groups. Instead of that, we will review some potential official and non-violent reactions of developing countries, to counter the endless global growing gap situation, being experienced by them. This reflection will be done "not to give ideas" to some developing countries, on how to offset economic frustrations but to provide the Western players with some clues of what they could encounter along their wrong path.

To begin with, we will refer here to a *ceteris paribus* likely increase in the frequency of skirmishes[147] or economic battles among the different players, the rich and the developing countries. And this

---

147. One of these skirmishes has taken place recently in a leading developing country, India. This country has in the spring of 2003 decided to refuse bilateral development grants and loans, the amount of which are small in terms of own GDP and implementation of is time consuming, as they are highly conditioned. This was an expected decision as India itself gives almost a similar amount of aid to neighbouring countries and clearly shows its willingness to become a global political player.

starting from the present situation, which is one of fatigue and irritation among leaderships of developing countries, after years of greedy behaviour concerning development financing and a practical deadlock in international trade negotiations[148]. Even recently the rich countries have remained aloof to the call for better behaviour of the West made by the "Non Align Movement"[149]in their last meeting. At this meeting remembrance of the dark times of colonialism reappeared and messages on exploitation of LDC, currently practised by rich countries in the name of market freedom, were also undertone.

5.4.3.1. Weakening of multilateralism and rise of trade regionalism

We do believe that in the future, the formation or deepening of trade agreements at regional level, in the absence of multilateral progress and in the search for additional regional trade gains, could be more rules than exception. To the extent that in the next ten years, and as a reaction from frustrations, regionalism continues prevailing over multilateralism the global trade gains will result sub-optimal[150]. Observe that although the current tendency towards regionalism is constantly criticised within WTO by officials, we have to certify that, despite its sub-optimality, this non-multilateral behaviour has always been at the playground, enhanced among others by the European Union. Note additionally that this trade regionalism, as a midway between bilateralism and multilateralism, is completely legal in the context of WTO rules.

Even more, one should not rule out the possibility that relevant developing countries from one moment onwards invoke some

---

148. In relation with negotiations of the WTO, the main source of criticism made by the developing countries to the West, has been the lack of "implementation" of the pledges made in the Uruguay Round, in relation with agriculture and services. According to these commitments, developing countries would reduce their industrial tariff duties, in a phased way, in exchange for a meaningful improvement in access to Western markets in the field of agriculture, garments, and services. Although they have not fulfilled their commitments in the previous Round, the Western countries have once again put pressure to launch another Round at the Ministerial Conference in Doha.

149. Sessions celebrated in Kuala Lumpur (Malaysia) in the third week of February 2003.

150. The solution towards encouraging regional trade cannot be optimal. This is because the formation of trade blocs is prone to induce the so called "trade diversion" from the cheapest sources, and to increase the intra-bloc commerce, the so called "trade creation" by the artificial means of keeping external common tariffs while eliminating the internal ones.

principles of the GATT rules, for diverting a number of relevant western export products. Western countries should acknowledge that an eventual unleashing of such manoeuvres could be disruptive for the evolution of their GDP[151]. Depending on the duration of the action, the number of involved countries and the number of diverted items, a sudden turning point in the western economic business cycle could be forced.

It is clear that in economic wars there are no absolute gainers, while in fair economic co-operation long-term gains for all is the expected solution. Notwithstanding that, the country or group of countries that called for the war (selecting the ground and the moment for initiation) may lose less than those that have to react. In particular when their internal cycles are to some extent de-coupled from those of the West because their economies are large (in PPP terms) and less dependent. The countries that initiate war could even gain, if all sides finally acknowledge the departure position as unfair.

Consequently a more positive approach of western countries in current trade negotiations should be enhanced by means of modifying their *quid pro quo* behaviour. This strategy, apparently more profitable for them at short-term, will work in the long run against the interest of rich countries and could make the global economy more unstable.

5.4.3.2. Uncertainty and economic stagnation as likely results

Letting aside eventual cyclical recoveries, a continuation of actions of international terrorism or the above depicted trade strategies could lead to a global situation of sluggish development, stagnation or even something worse, created by the persistence of uncertainty. This uncertainty would hover round the main economic players, arresting their investment plans and general prosperity. In such a situation, it is not likely that Western countries opt to retaliate by invading economic-rival countries, given the fact that some of these countries, are almost continents, densely populated and with powerful armies, which makes almost impossible to occupy them by

---

151. The West should bear in mind that as early as 2009, four larger developing countries (China India, Brazil and Russia) could generate an additional expenditure larger than that of the so called G-6 Group (US, France, Germany, Italy, Japan and U.K.). Goldman-Sachs (2003) Global Paper 99. 1st October.

comparable small although high-tech armies. And if by chance a partial occupancy became a reality, public opinion in western countries could undermine the biased economic foundations (neo-colonialism) of this occupation.

If a significant commercial war starts, it is likely that a political one follows in the arena of international institutions. If this be the case, it is also possible that most international economic institutions would lose track because in such a situation they would become useless[152]. In this context, even if the former international economic institutions would remain, alternative institutions for regional or inter-regional trade and financing could appear. This would not be a very recommendable situation, but a possible result of short-sightedness of rich countries. Although the mentioned regionalism in trade and finance is by itself a sub-optimum solution, developing countries could consider it as positive in comparison to the former biased one.

5.5. The role of the UN in this context

Since the UN and its agencies, besides involvement in conflict resolution (Security Council) and other political issues, also have to devise global economic policies, one could wonder what would happen with the UN in the above-described hypothetical context. If as a result of failures, some specialised agencies of the UN and the WTO enter into a process of bifurcation, one could not put much hope for the continuation of the UN as a neutral mechanism for solving international economic and political problems.

This bifurcation could result from the feeling of a lack of representation of interests of developing countries in f.i. IMF and World Bank, or could occur due to deadlock in WTO negotiations. Note that this hypothetical bifurcation is more probable now than 30 years ago when the so-called North–South conflict emerged in the UN without a significant disruption. This probability is higher, not only because the economic gap has significantly grown, or the IT

---

152. If finally a commercial war starts between developing and rich countries, and its virulence is significant, by its temporal dimension and/or by the number of involved countries, the bankruptcy of the WTO is almost guaranteed. Additionally, if a significant number of developing countries abandon the WTO, this would also undermine the IMF.

revolution has generalised access to information, but also because the economic and political world-structure has changed dramatically. Countries like China and India are geographically a huge part of the planet with respectively a maximum or high growth rate, have a vast majority of the global population and keep a trend for more intense political and economic co-operation among them.

In our view, however, this potentially negative development concerning multilateral institutions would not deteriorate without reactions of some Western and some advanced developing countries, which still believe in the efficiency and supremacy of multilateral action and international law. In this case, these countries would first arrest the decadence of the UN, and thereafter engage again into multilateralism by reforming the Charter.

6

Changes to Correct Current Trends

Towards a Global Welfare Society

Until now, we have tried to describe the evolution of the main traits of the economic and political relations among the different countries of the world. So far these relations have to a great extent been based on the political and economic strength historically cumulated by different countries, mainly since the Modern Age, in which some modern empires (mainly Spain, France, Britain, and Portugal) took shape. Thereafter, some overseas parts of these empires emerged as independent and potentially rich nations, as the US, and others for long remained attached to the old colonial power (Australia and Canada).

Spain was the first modern empire that lost almost all its colonies. In the 19th Century, Germany and Italy appeared as new European countries, which in order to compete with the rest of the leaders started their own colonial expansion. Without spectacular historical actions, around 1870, The Netherlands focussing mainly on international trade, became the richest country of the world in terms of per capita income. Note that the Scandinavian countries were a part of Europe, wherein the need for overseas expansion was less pressing, thus resulting in long periods without costly wars. This circumstance, combined with plentiful natural resources and scant demographic pressure, gave them the possibility of silently becoming rich.

Outside of the European continent, Japan, from the 19th Century onwards, was the first Asian country involved in modern expansionist policies, similar to that practised by some European powers. Russia that had long before started its territorial expansion in Central Asia, was the only additional player to count with. Most colonised countries, and others that remained far away from the relevant axis of international trade, were more or less forced to remain underdeveloped.

The different political and military strength among players of the two layers (colonisers and colonised), conditioned from the very beginning the economic relations among them, which usually were not only uneven but at times unfair and based on serfdom. Much later, in the 19th Century, the development of a liberal economic model that was based on the core idea of free interchange, improved the old inefficient trade relations among the big players. However, although the relationship between colonising powers and colonies underwent some formal changes, practically they maintained the previous traits of inequality.

In Chapter 2 we have depicted the evolution of the economic philosophy underlying the applied model by western countries. Letting aside the first two-thirds of the 19th century in which a hangover of mercantilism continued, one should recognise that since 1870 a growing but fluctuating freedom to interchange took place. Nonetheless we must underline that the successive applied approaches have since then remained far from a correct interpretation of the so-called neo-classical model. Consequently, one cannot say *strictu sensu* that the applied approach in international economic relations since 1870 has been one of a free market, but an approach with variable and selected degrees of freedom administered by ruling powers.

On the other hand, one should not forget that an economic model of total freedom, as the purely neo-classical one, generates divers income distribution positions according to the initial differences in ownership of technology and resources among players.

Observe that the initial geographical distribution of resources at the moment of the Industrial Revolution was not very fair due to colonialism. Consequently, the evolution of income distribution results of the model had to be unsatisfactory and deficient, as reality has proved. This deficiency has been especially perceivable in the recent era of globalisation. Indeed, with the exception of the so-called "golden age", in which the regional disparity of per capita income shrank, the history of the last two centuries is a history of a growing economic disparity between rich and poor regions.

After the Second World War, the UN established some international economic institutions to pursue, among others, the correction of the growing distribution imbalance. However, for different reasons as analysed above, neither the IMF, nor the World

Bank, nor the WTO have been able to devise effective policies for bridging the gap and to sufficiently correct the intrinsic dysfunction of the ruling approach of the neo-classical model.

Additionally, in the last decades, the evolution of political philosophy has also conditioned the relations between the rich and poor, be these individuals or nations. Current Darwinism and short-term consumerism have impregnated life and opinion in the rich world, in which the aim of a radical short-term economic efficiency has provisionally gain prominence over social justice and long-term efficiency.

However the traits of the nuke economic reality, and the recent events motivated by poverty, ignorance, hatred and exclusion, seem to contradict that efficiency, as it is currently understood, should continue being the sole goal in economic relations, with oblivion of greater equity. We opine that in a global well informed society, future additional increase in the economic gap or even its maintenance is not only non-recommendable, but also inconsistent with a long-term efficiency approach, and consequently inconsistent with global stability, prosperity, and peace.

6.1. In search of sustainable growth, social justice and peace for all

From our perspective, the final aims to be achieved by mankind in the next two decades or within one generation, are global peace and human security. These are two international public goods that can only be reached by implementation of some global policies, which will have to act as intermediate goals. These intermediate objectives, mainly economic in nature, such as significantly bridging the economic gap by means of reconsideration of development financing, the renewal of WTO rules to create fairer international trade, or an agreement on movements of people, will have to take place in a multilateral context.

In a similar way, a fairer and multilateral approach is required for the political solution of long-lasting and burning problems, such as those of the Middle East and the Great Lake area in Africa. This multilateral approach has no alternatives since in our world today it is unthinkable that relevant regional conflicts have no negative spill-over effects elsewhere.

As we do believe that the key for future resolution of general problems of humanity is to treat them mainly in a multilateral context, it is necessary to urgently reorganise the UN, which is the "per excellence" multilateral institution we have.

Nevertheless we should not forget that the UN in its current shape, from the time of its inception with the choice of New York[153] as its headquarter, up to the last created committee in our days, basically has followed a step by step alluvium accumulation process. It is true that there have been several attempts to reorganise the UN and its specialised agencies, but these attempts have not fructified perhaps by their lack of opportunity, and the suffocating rules for change contained in its Charter.

6.1.1. Changing the UN is urgent

In our view and for several political and economic reasons[154], the moment for a drastic change in the UN has finally arrived. The world cannot go ahead without resolving the most important problems that hinder the implementation of relevant and pending objectives[155], or without changing the UN decision-making process, including voting systems in different organs. This should be done in order to reform the formation of the will of the institution and to correct its democratic deficit.

Besides, a UN that is not operative enough to solve the economic and political problems of our global village deserves neither its present budget (which is very small) nor any additional comment. Good intentions or mere political tactics are not enough to solve problems. We should not create or keep organs alive with inadequate financing for the functions assigned to them. This only generates

---

153. Note that the geographically non-centred city of New York was chosen as headquarter of UN at a time in which the ruling insecurity in Europe or North Africa did not allow to establish headquarter in this area, which is the gravity centre of international traffic. Besides, placing the UN headquarter in the economic capital of the hegemonic power does not appear to be neutral.

154. We here refer to the breaking down of the old political equilibrium at times of the cold war, and the growing gap.

155. To reach the final objective (international public goods) it is necessary to boost, pool and reorganise the future transfer of funds from the rich countries to the poor ones, and to do it under the aegis of the UN. Other basic multilateral institutions as the IMF should also undergo significant corrections. The WTO should also look for another methodology for negotiations, more in favour of the LDC, and detached from the current *quid pro quo* approach.

frustrations. For instance, the function of stimulating the development of LDC, committed in the Charter of the UN, cannot be achieved by just making minimal investments[156], as for long the developed countries has been prone to believe in opposition to the corollaries of the theory of economic growth. Much more finance for development is absolutely necessary to avoid future problems related with peace and security.

The current scant development aid budget of around 0.23% of donors GDP is spent partly in bilateral programmes and partly via multilateral institutions. In the past decade multilateral funding has gained ground over the bilateral, fragmented and over-conditioned one. This more desirable trend, in parallel with an indispensable multiplication of funds devoted to this activity, requires the reorganisation of the UN, the only institution capable of facilitating the achievement of the above mentioned international public goods.

Concerning this reorganisation, we think that it would be preferable not to compromise on current privileges of the powerful (thus degrading democracy), since this would be in demerit of the main final aims. In this regard it would be preferable to have a UN with less represented countries rather than all represented, but some of them taking advantage of the decision making process in their own interest. Nevertheless we believe that the current privileged countries will finally accept a new non-privileged status instead of remaining outside of multilateral management of world developments[157].

6.1.2. On the main traits of a programme for global stability

Summarising, we do believe that the main directives of a programme for global stability and institutional reform, which is the core aim of this essay, would be the following:

1) Restructuring and updating the UN, implementing a new Charter for, among others, solving the current problem of its

---

156. Note that the allocation of resources to this activity by the donors, including multilateral institutions, today reach the ridiculous figure of the 0.23% of GDP of donor countries, as compared to the UN proposed 0.7% in the 70s.

157. Note that a new UN with effective control on commercial flows, via resolutions on embargoes, extra-tariffs applicable to non member states etc, could introduce stimuli for proper behaviour of powerful but reluctant countries.

democratic deficit. This would include establishing a new global compulsory funding system based on the principle of the ability to pay of the different members, and a parallel mechanism for expelling persistent debtors, but also establishing new activities, in particular the top administration of a new development programme (UNICO).

2) Reconsideration of the recommended economic measures supplied by the Washington Consensus, taking into account some of the problems we have detected in Chapter 2 and the financial needs of LDC for catching up. In this regard the currently selected neo-classical corollaries for market liberalisation should be reassessed, in particular concerning freer movements of labour at an international scale. Likewise the current sequencing of liberalisation should be restated;

3) Establishment of a real commitment for public foreign financing of LDC, in order to significantly bridge the economic gap in a generation, and to push up the poorest countries at a level of per capita GDP around 3100 US dollars (of the year 2002) in 2030;

4) Establishing a real commitment on sustainability (climate change, demography, water management, and food and health security) in consistency with bridging the gap;

5) Reorganisation of an effective conflict resolution system and creation of a UN defence system for early warning and rapid intervention.

6.2. Means for reaching the former aims

Knowing the final aims of our essay and having outlined the main intermediate objectives of our programem, we will now enter into details on these intermediate targets and instruments, which will allow the working of our proposals.

6.2.1. Reorganisation of the UN

As mentioned in the above paragraphs, the UN would be the core institution to implement our proposals for achieving the mentioned international public goods. However, here we will only enter into the description of the indispensable reforms of the UN and some of its agencies (mainly Security Council, and IMF and WB). Logically we will not enter into comments on restructuring the rest of the complex UN organisation (special agencies, committees, and other bodies).

In our opinion to achieve peace and security, a twofold strategy is required. On the one hand bridging the economic gap and on the other solving current conflicts and preventing future political and economic snags. As a consequence, it will be indispensable to modify the Security Council, including its rules for membership and voting system. Although some may believe that corrections in the office of the Secretary General are vital, we will not deal with this issue as it does not form the core of our proposals. Since our focus on the UN capabilities in the 21st century is much more ambitious than the historical one, the issues on the UN and its financial problems will also be taken up. In particular the proposed UNICO and its institutional framework will be described in detail.

6.2.1.1. The Security Council and its reform

The first issue to be discussed here is that of membership and, as a derivative, the regional representation in the Security Council. At this moment the structure of the Security Council is one that is still rooted in the outcome of the Second World War with the victors as permanent members of the Council (Russia, US, France, UK and China[158]). In addition there are ten members in rotation every two years, proposed by the General Assembly.

It is clear that this international body has serious problems concerning democratic global representation. The current small number of members, necessary to gain efficiency according to the existing Charter, makes it easy for some permanent members to buy wills in exchange for financial or political promises. Thus our call for increasing the number of member countries represented to 24. A fixed number per continent or region, according to its political and

---

158. At the moment of inception of the Security Council, a civil war was going on in the Republic of China. In 1949 Mao Tze Dong took power in mainland China, while the nationalist government flew to Taiwan. Between 1946 and 1971 the Chinese seat in the Security Council was occupied by the so-called Republic of China (Taiwan) and not by People's Republic of China (Continental China).

economic importance should make up this representation[159]. This would be the only way to obtain a more balanced geographical representation[160], more regional co-operation and less dominance of current permanent members.

In the second place the membership of the Security Council could be divided in two categories: long term membership (f.i. 10 years tenure), extracted from most prominent countries of every region, and short term membership (two years) extracted from the rest, and the latter also selected on a regional basis. This would imply the disappearance of permanent membership, which having been logical in the cold-war era does not seem relevant[161] today. A tentative distribution of seats between long tenure and short tenure could be 8 and 16 respectively.

Thirdly, concerning the decision-making process, all members of the Security Council should have a vote with the same value, and resolutions should be passed by qualified majorities (for instance two-thirds) and in a fixed time-span. This would imply the disappearance of veto rights, an institution established for consensus building that has proved not to be the most effective for attaining peace and security but rather paralysing. It is remarkable that of around 1700 proposed resolutions in the past 50 years in the Security Council, almost 250 were vetoed (15%) based on the self-interest of one or more vetoing permanent members. At the same

---

159. End May 2003 the British Prime Minister, in trying to repair the inflicted damage to the Security Council by the UK and US, suggested some changes in this body. Specifically he suggested the inclusion of Japan, Germany, India and Brazil as new permanent members, while the body would enlarge up to 24 members. As one could expect his enlargement proposal did not suggest eliminating the veto right of permanent member in the Security Council, thus further complicating decision making in the Council. Note that this could create a more prone atmosphere for unilateral actions.

160. Nowadays China is the only Third World and only Asian country among the permanent members of the Security Council. At the same time Germany and Japan contribute much more financially to the UN than Russia, China, UK and France, without playing a minimum role.

161. The Charter is extremely inflexible and non democratic in terms of decision making for Charter reforms. In article 108 of the Charter it is written "Amendments to the present Charter shall come into force ... when they have been adopted by a vote of two-thirds of the members of the General Assembly and ratified in accordance with their respective constitutional processes by two-thirds ..., including all the permanent members of the Security Council". These last 9 words are, in our view, an entire defy to the logic of democracy. Opting for maintaining the decision making structure as devised in 1945 will avert rational updating.

time quite a number of adopted resolutions were not implemented. All this means that the Security Council has to be reformed as soon as possible to provide an effective and manifold resolution system when peace and human security are threatened or have entered into a situation of breaking down.

6.2.1.2. On the financial problems of the UN

As one can deduce from economic theory and history, without enough multilateral funds the world will not be able to push its peace and security agenda forward with a minimum of rationality[162]. Consequently, if the UN wants to overcome the development financing problems of LDC; to become more fair and efficient in its voting processes; and to be the core institution for promoting international public goods, the amount of contributions from member states, has to be multiplied substantially.

The current regular UN funding includes budgets for the administration, major organs and auxiliary agencies, and programmes. Peacekeeping expenses have a separate budget, as do the specialised agencies (including World Bank, IMF). These three types of expenditures (regular budget, peacekeeping, and specialised agencies) are funded by membership contributions according to a formula based on the principle of the ability to pay. However many economic and social programmes of the specialised agencies (such as UNICEF, UNESCO and WHO) are funded by voluntary contributions of member states.

Concerning its evolution and size, the total expenditure of the UN hardly doubled in the period 1986-1996, reaching an amount of around 13 billion dollars[163] in 1996. An insignificant and disputed figure that by itself expresses the intrinsic incapability of the current UN to solve the basic problems of the world assigned to them. With this volume of funds one cannot expect much more than exerting the right to talk and listen.

The assessed formula for contribution made by member countries to finance the three mentioned types of expenditures, is

---

162. Rahman, RD and Andreu, JM. (2002a: 49) Financing Economic Development..., book already mentioned.

163. Mingst, K. and Karns, M. (2000: 40), book already mentioned.

evaluated every three years according to the members GDP, their per capita GDP, their ability to obtain foreign currencies, besides other additional pointers. At the inception of the UN, the US paid 40% of the regular budget, while now it only pays 22 %. The minimum assessed rate was initially 0.04% for the poorest developing countries, but now this figure is just 0.001%[164].

In the wake of these figures we have to underline that the current assessed funding is in need of a radical modification because its structure, being unfair and inefficient, occasionally prompts non democratic behaviour of some members. We could additionally illustrate the financial mess of the UN by clarifying that at this moment 88 UN members, slightly less than a simple majority, all together pay less than 1% of the assessed budgets. Conversely, of the 5 top contributors, *US, Japan, Germany, France, and UK*, who finance around two-thirds of the budgets, 3 are permanent members of the Security Council and the rest (Japan and Germany) only pay for the party.

Leaving aside the scant available resources and the unbalanced assessed funding, the UN also has to deal with confirmed debtors. In fact in September 1998, many member states owned to the UN over 2.5 billion dollars for current and past assessments. Surprisingly only 100 of the then 185 members were not in arrears. In those days the US was the biggest debtor, owing two-thirds of the outstanding credits of the UN[165], and according to some detractors it used this default to boycott policies it was not in favour of.

6.2.1.3. Manipulation of the UN by superpowers

A great level of partisanship and clientelism has been patent along the entire trajectory of the UN. Initially till the 70s, the US used the UN and its agencies for legitimisation of its own actions, and for blocking actions of others, as did the Soviet Union. Also note that, concurrently, the US did highly influence the rule-enforcing and

---

164. We have some doubts on the efficiency of the allocation of resources, created by the case of being a member of a club without paying practically anything. Similarly the situation in which one member (out of 185) pays 22% of the budget is not desirable because it creates strong vested interest and lack of neutrality in organs.

165. Mingst, K. and Karns, M. (2000: 42), book already mentioned.

economic policies of the Bretton Wood institutions (IMF, World Bank), while it often contradicted the principles of the WTO.

In the 70s and 80s, a growing number of members (developing countries), succeeded in using the UN for coalition building, undermining the dominance of the US. In those days the developing countries, by demanding a new international economic order (NIEO), constantly put the US in a defensive position. In reaction to this, instead of realising a platform for dialogue and a search for consensus, the US rather preferred withdrawal from some crucial organisations such as ILO (International Labour Organisation) and UNESCO, thus blocking its assessed contribution[166].

Years later, after the fall of the Berlin Wall, the US recovered its position as the major player in the UN, thus reflecting its new hegemonic role at the global stage. In the 90s the US approach of using the UN and specialised agencies for its own international policies (in particular the activities of IMF and World Bank) has increased. This does not imply that the US is the only nation that is profiting from its special position in the UN. France, UK and Russia as a result of their permanent membership in the Security Council, also benefit from their positions.

As a consequence of the recent polarisation of power, and in the absence of radical reforms of the UN and its affiliates, these organisations will not be able to work significantly for common interest, nor to contribute to the achievement of the wanted international public goods. In our view, the only way to unlock the current power play and its doubtful outcomes for peace and security is to restrain the power policy of the current hegemonic power by means of creating constructive countervailing powers capable of devising a new balance in the Security Council. In the short-term one could visualise the possibility of the appearance of different countervailing powers. One such a power could emerge from the formation of a European Federation (a voluntary federation formed by several homogeneous European states). There is also the possibility that a new block of common interest emerges in Euro-Asia (India, China and Russia).

---

166. Mingst, K. and Karns, M. (2000: 49), book already mentioned.

6.2.2. Reconsideration of the applied multilateral economic policies

To guarantee the efficiency of the new UN-institution (UNICO) for promoting development[167], two initiatives have to be accomplished: 1) a serious reconsideration of the till now specific applications of the neo-classical model; and 2) a revision of the policy recommendations of the Bretton Woods institutions and a change in the WTO approach for negotiation. This is because past policy recommendations and ways of negotiation of these institutions have resulted in an untenable growing economic gap (vide Chapter 3).

6.2.2.1. Velocity and sequencing of the applied policies

In Chapter 2 we have discussed the specific policy applications of the triumphant neo-classical model in the last decades. In our view the followed approach was either wrong in its formulation, or was intentionally devised to improve the relative position of the rich countries. In any case its outcome has not reduced the economic gap among regions.

In particular we have discussed in Chapter 2 the lack of professional knowledge on the dynamics of the optimisation when non-competitive economies move towards free markets. Neither history nor economic theory has provided us with safe instruments to choose the length of the period of transition to optimise the results of the process. However, history has proven that the periods for successful transition have been longer than half a decade or even a decade, this in contradiction to the recommendations of the Bretton Woods institutions (Washington Consensus) which are in favour of hasty liberalisation.

An additional failure in the adopted strategy by the Washington Consensus, concerning the development of LDC, has been the order or "sequencing" of policies to be implemented so that the different markets can be liberalised in an efficient way. After the development of a basic infrastructure, which mainly has to be financed with (foreign) public funds, the next policy to be implemented in developing countries to gain productivity and efficiency in allocation of resources, should be the liberalisation of international trade. An increase in FDI can only be expectable thereafter.

---

167. UNICO stands for UN Institution for Co-operation.

In this regard it is not justifiable that rich countries forget the liberalisation of their markets for agricultural goods and services, while at the same time they push for a freer access of industrial goods and FDI to markets in developing countries, in order to increase their own business opportunities.

Even worse, whenever Western countries are questioned about the liberalisation of the labour market or the freedom of movement of people, they normally insist that the ILO should handle this issue, and that it should not be raised in WTO negotiations. Paradoxically rich countries, instead of recommending the management of the issues of environment or (child) labour conditions to specialised agencies such as UNEP or ILO, they have unduly brought these issues to WTO. This disputable allocation of means and entities to ends reflects the power play in the Bretton Woods institutions and the WTO.

One should not forget that the professional economists in management positions in these institutions have never considered a two-way (South-North and *vice versa*) freer international labour mobility as a main issue to achieve general international welfare. Note that this asymmetry is similar to the others mentioned in relation to international trade negotiations, and is based on a short-sighted self interest of the West. Even more, this asymmetric practise is against the basic corollary of the neo-classical model concerning freedom of movement of factors to gain efficiency, as Bretton Woods institutions have always recommended inside the boundaries of western countries to gain welfare.

No wonder that the wrong sequencing in the liberalisation process and the defective allocation of instruments[168] for meeting ends became what we have witnessed, thus driving the economies to a growing gap, and not *vice versa*.

---

168. Note that in the WTO the decision making process is not based on the importance of different countries (weighted voting, typical for the Bretton Wood institutions) but on the rule of consensus. Given the fact that this rule of consensus does not admit solutions to improve positions of the more in demerit of the few, who logically will exercise their veto rights, this rule will be normally conducive to paralysing procedures in decision making. As a consequence, although to some extent the rule of consensus is more democratic than the weighted voting in accordance with economic importance, it is less democratic than the simple rule of majority of represented population. No wonder that as a result of this rule of consensus, multilateral significant advances are not expectable. Consensus among groups of neighbouring countries to form regional trade blocs is more likely, thus protracting current trends in international trade.

6.2.2.2. Necessary and sufficient conditions once again

In Chapter 2 we have also discussed the difference between the necessary and the sufficient conditions to obtain a projected outcome. In that Chapter we also reviewed the so-called necessary conditions that, according to the Washington Consensus, should be present to make economic progress in developing countries and their economic catching up possible. Assessing the validity of these conditions for development we have deduced from empirical evidence that they are neither necessary nor sufficient.

One could here remember the economic environment of the "golden age" of capitalism, a Keynesian and interventionist period. We can easily deduce that most countries could grow in this period without fulfilling some of the assumed "necessary" conditions of the Washington Consensus (such as almost nil inflation, balanced public sector, free internal and external markets, and so on). On the other hand some of the truly necessary conditions for growth at catching up rhythm[169] are not even explicitly mentioned in the conditions-recipe of the Washington Consensus.

We are convinced that the command structure of the Bretton Wood institutions (WB, IMF) is well aware of the differences between the necessary and the sufficient conditions for growth. Therefore we cannot understand as to why they are ignoring the negative economic facts derived by the implementation in the 90s of their own recipes.

In relation to stepping up the economic growth rate of developing countries, which would be necessary to achieve the international public goods mentioned above, professional economists knew already half a century[170] ago that the increase in the domestic investment rate and its financing (with internal and external savings) is crucial. In this regard we should not forget that the countries that have in the last 50 years grown at extraordinary rates (catching up rates), have been more exception than rule.

---

169. A sufficient domestic investment rate will only be achievable in most of LDC if public foreign transfers enter significantly to reinforce small internal savings.

170. The Harrod-Domar model that was the first mathematical formalisation of the growth process started from the idea that the only scant factor is physical capital. The model established the equilibrium conditions in the goods and service markets and in the labour market. Although this growth model is the most elemental one, it is still roughly valid and continues being explained in all the handbooks of Macroeconomics. Note that this model was presented by R. Harrod in 1936.

Cases such as Japan, South Korea, Taiwan, Hong Kong and Singapore (the case of China has been rather exceptional)[171], which have registered growth rates of around 7-8 % for long periods, have received important net financial contributions from external sources. However, this does not imply that improving the accessibility of internal markets to FDI, one of the elements of the conditions of the Washington Consensus, may automatically provoke the massive arrival of FDI and the acceleration of growth. The experience of progressive liberalisation processes of capital movements in the 90s, and its meagre outcomes in most LDC in terms of GDP growth rate, proves that many conditions for growth of the Washington Consensus are neither necessary nor sufficient.

To the extent that the catching up process requires high rates of domestic investments, and given the fact that LDC cannot count with enough domestic savings, they necessarily have to resort to foreign capital, be this public or private. In this context of scant financing, if private flows to LDC (mainly FDI) are not significant, catching up would require public external financing. Even more, to entrust the entire process of acceleration of domestic investment to the private (internal or external) sector would be overlooking the historical reality of the economy of many poor countries, even in the 90s.

6.3. Reorganisation of public external financing for development

As we have mentioned before, the development financing of LDC does not only depend on their domestic savings, but also on their ability to raise foreign savings in order to increase their domestic rate of investment. Note that these foreign savings must be equivalent to the current account balance (but with the opposite sign). Since most LDC present deficits in their current accounts, this means that they receive foreign capital in net terms. As far as developing countries are concerned the three most important items to raise foreign savings have historically been the FDI, the so-called private "portfolio investments", and the Official Assistance to Development (ODA).

------

171. The case of China is rather exceptional because its huge ratio domestic savings/ GDP has for years been higher than the ratio domestic investment/GDP, thus enabling the accrual of an enormous volume of foreign reserves. Note that over a long period of time, this increase in foreign reserves has been larger than the received FDI.

6.3.1. Recent evolution of FDI in external financing of LDC

It is well known that in the 90s there has been an upside-down movement between FDI and ODA, with the former surpassing the ODA by a great extent, while the latter entered into a situation of nominal stagnation. To be specific, FDI received by developing countries have experienced a rapid increase in the last decades, in particular in the last one[172], reaching the unexpected and enormous figure of 185 billion US dollars in 1999. Although these growth rates of FDI could have worked along the line predicted by the Washington Consensus, the naked truth is that 60% of this FDI has gone to Asia, and 30% to China. To this concentrated regional distribution of FDI we could add that in 1997 a total of 9 developing countries received 71% of the total investment efforts deployed by multinational corporations[173]. On the other hand and conversely, the African countries as a whole received less than 3% of the total FDI, and the 29 poorest countries received less than 2%.

Truly, this distribution of FDI, which is geographically unbalanced, completely matches with the logic of the free market. The risk of losing capital put at stake will be higher in LDC with serious problems of foreign indebtedness, insufficient infrastructure, or socio-political problems. No wonder that multinational corporations, trying to obtain maximum profits in the short term, invest 80-90% of their foreign flows in industrialised countries, and the rest exclusively in developing countries with the highest current and foreseeable growth rates.

6.3.2. Recent evolution of short-term capital flows to LDC

The interest of LDC in the new arrival of foreign capital in order to complement domestic savings does not end with attempts to attract FDI. They may also have interest in drawing "private portfolio investments". Note that these portfolio investments have experienced a similar fast rhythm of growth in a major period of the past decade, 1990-2000[174]. Both the progressive opening of real markets in

---

172. The FDI received by developing countries, amounting up to 2.4 billion US dollars in 1962, multiplied its volume in 2 decades, reaching the figure of US $ 11 billion in 1980. Later in the 80s, the volume of FDI doubled again, and finally in the 90s its volume multiplied again by more than 4.
173. Todaro, M. (2003: 635), book already mentioned.
174. Todaro, M. (2003: 645), book already mentioned.

developing countries to foreign investors and the pervasive liberalisation of internal financial markets in these countries have unleashed significant growth of private portfolio investments. At the end of the last century, "portfolio investments" made up one quarter of the total foreign savings received by developing countries[175].

Assessing the contribution of "foreign portfolio investment" to the development of these countries, we have to say that, from a static point of view, free movements of capital will increase the welfare level of all participants, as it has been concluded many times by professional economists[176]. However from the perspective of the economic policy practised by developing countries, it is crucial to establish how volatile these portfolio investments can be. If these investments (shares or public debt) are not stable, they may be more prejudicial than beneficial.

Consequently we could say that developing countries that do rely heavily on these inflows for financing their development, are more prone to capital market instability than others, and may often suffer enormous financial complications in their economic policy. In general, short-term capital can only help those LDC with a stable economy, a sound currency, a sound fiscal administration and banking system, and steady growth. These traits, although top-listed as "necessary" conditions for attracting private foreign capital by the Washington Consensus in order to enable economic catching up, unfortunately are not very common in most LDC[177].

---

175. Between 1990 and 1999, the total portfolio investments realised in developing countries multiplied around 12 times, reaching the figure of US dollars 60 billion. Note that multinational pension funds, special hedge funds, big international mutual funds, and other institutional savers and investors of the industrialised countries entered in the 90s in this business in order to develop a strategy of international diversification of their portfolio.

176. To explain this movement of capital towards developing countries, it is necessary that the returns of capital in these countries are higher than that of the industrialised ones. But sometimes, in some critical moments, the economic situation of the recipient crumbles so quickly that the value of shares slumps and the foreign capital suddenly flows back to the countries of origin, generating a deep perturbation (including an over-reaction) in the value of the currency of the involved country. This means that the temporal stability of these external savings is at times very scant.

177. When developing countries experience an economic shock, or a negative expectation of a slump in stock exchange prices, short-term capital that had been previously received, with its flowing out, may accentuate the problem, unless a tax on speculative capital is implemented.

6.3.3. Recent evolution of ODA and its irrational distribution

An alternative source of foreign funds in order to increase the total available foreign savings is Official Development Assistance (ODA) also called Foreign Aid. Note that the pejorative content of the words "assistance" and "aid" clearly reveal the intentions of the donors during the past 50 years. They just marginally funded certain investments or even food, many a times based on a mix of charity and export promotion, without any implicit or explicit intention of effectively stimulating economic catching up of the poorest countries.

The current value of ODA, directed towards developing countries and LDC, which includes bilateral and multilateral grants or loans, as well as technical assistance, has grown in absolute terms from US 4.6 billion in 1960, to a magnitude of around US 50 billion in 2002. However if we compare the current value of total foreign aid with total GDP of donor countries, we can conclude that the international ODA has shown a continuous decline from 0.51% registered in 1960 to 0.24% in 1999[178] (0.23% in 2001). Already in 1971 the UN established a target figure of 0.7% of donor GDP as a minimum, based on the successful experience with the Marshall Plan. Note however that along all these years only a few countries have reached this 0.7% GDP target, namely Denmark, Norway, the Netherlands and Sweden.

In relation to the sources, we can say that although Japan and the US remain being the most important donors in absolute terms, the case of the US is rather disappointing. The amount of its foreign aid is relatively very low in terms of its GDP (0.1%), and strongly tinted with geo-political targets and not with the idea of bridging the gap. Observe that for years the US annually invested more than 1% of its GDP in the Marshall Plan to rebuild Europe, and that this effort was profitable for both sides. Considering that the presently felt insecurity generated by poverty-driven international terrorism is somewhat similar to the insecurity generated by the fear for communist take-overs in Europe at the dawn of the cold war, one wonders why the US today is not willing to effectively boost its

---

178. Perkins, D. *et al.* (2001: 409) Economics of Development. 5th Edition. Norton.

development financing directed to LDC[179]. Undoubtedly this strategy would again be mutually profitable, would increase global security and not in the least improve the deteriorating image of the US.

What is more revealing about the chaotic situation of current ODA is its arbitrary and irrational distribution among the developing countries. In terms of regional distribution, we can say that although nearly 50% of the world's poorest live in Asia, this continent receives only 3 US dollars per capita per annum. This is in sharp contrast to the Middle East (i.p. Israel and Egypt), where the received per capita foreign aid is six times the per capita aid rate in South Asia. And this while the per capita income in the Middle East is five times higher than that of South Asia, which reveals that this so-called aid is basically an instrument of geopolitics. Similarly East Europe and Central Asia, with more than four times the per capita income of Sub Saharan Africa receives more aid than the Sub Saharan countries.

If we consider the distribution of foreign aid by individual developing countries, and not by regions or subcontinents, the relation between geographical allocation of foreign aid and the level of poverty, is also amazing. To cite an example we could say that only 31% of foreign aid is allocated to the 10 developing countries in which 66% of the poorest people of the world live, while 40% rather well off developing countries receive the double in per capita terms. To finalise this order of irrationalities we could add that those developing countries that spend more on military activities (over 4% of GDP) receive twice as much foreign aid in per capita terms as compared to LDC that spend less on defence.

One of the biggest additional problems of foreign aid in the last five decades has been the enormous fragmentation of the means of supplying funds. First of all, there is a fragmentation of institutions involved in the provision of aid (more than 20 multilateral institutions, around 40 bilateral donors, thousands of NGO's and so on). All these bodies have their own conditions, own priorities, own

---

179. Note that the huge financial transfers (in absolute terms) as recently agreed upon in US Congress are mainly directed to military operations (Afghanistan, Iraq) and post-war reconstruction. Note also that these increased financial transfers could partially act in demerit of others, directed to address tropical and poverty related diseases, as planned before.

accountability requirements and so on, which come along with a whole set of norms and red tape established in exchange for petty, fragmented and irrationally conditioned aid, thus paradoxically undermining national planning and good governance at the receiving end.

No wonder that a leading developing country as India has recently renounced to receive bilateral aid and concessional loans, since it considers the received ODA amounts as negligible[180] and the conditions exigent. All the above points out to the fact that the current ODA is squalid, whimsical and irrationally distributed, and not targeted towards bridging the gap.

6.3.4. *Non-substitutability of ODA and FDI in first stages*

Following the development process logic, private and public investments cannot, in general, substitute one another since the sequencing of their appearance into scene is not a matter of choice. Normally FDI flows to countries or enclaves when in these countries/ enclaves a sufficient infrastructure and healthy and educated manpower is available. Initially this enabling environment will have to be promoted by the public sector, since in this stage the private one would not significantly react, due to the fact that implicit demands for infrastructure, energy, education and so on, will not be accurately observable, as it happens with public goods. On the other hand, and as a consequence of the scant level of per capita GDP of these LDC, the demands for these goods would in any case be very small and artificially blurred by "free riders". Note that the small per capita GDP in LDC will neither generate sufficient domestic savings (in particular public savings), thus averting the possibility of sufficient public investment in the above mentioned sectors.

This generates a vicious circle, which would be almost impossible to break without resorting to public external capital. Conceptually, this external capital we are referring to, has the same public source (taxes levied from Western citizens) as the one that in other times financed the development of infrastructure and the welfare state in the western countries.

---

180. India received in 2000 an amount of aid around 0.2% of its GDP and around 1 dollar per person per year. Despite the above commented arguments over the amount and the conditions of the received aid, probably the desire of being consistent with the aspirations of India to play a role in global politics has also influenced the decision.

Summarising, we could say that for stepping up the economic development process in developing countries, in particular in LDC, it is necessary to increase the reception of foreign flows. However, the correct sequencing is to first receive public foreign transfers (currently ODA) in order to facilitate public investment in infrastructure and human capital, and only thereafter would it be rational to expect the arrival of significant FDI. A further opening of the internal market to international trade would also facilitate the arrival of FDI.

Note that the traditional ODA (bilateral, scant, non co-ordinated, without national targeting, and geo-politically directed) is a public source of foreign funds for LDC that should urgently be reorganised. In our view future amounts of public transfers to LDC should be increased, pooled and reshuffled under the aegis of the UN.

6.3.5. *Criticism on the functioning of ODA*

Along the last decade, high criticism concerning the effectiveness of the ODA has arisen and become dominant in the context of the Washington Consensus. The arguments for this criticism are manifold. One of the most frequently mentioned is the lack of good governance with focus on accountability and struggle against corruption. The second one is the "fashionable and radical" but wrong argument that practically all traditional public sector roles could be played in poor countries by the private sector. We should add a third alleged reason for limiting ODA, which is the scant absorption capacity, another assumed hindrance for reception of significant ODA. Last but not least we should mention the problem of substitution, also called fungibility[181].

In relation to the lack of accountability and the struggle against corruption, we have to say that this has probably been a typical trait of all public administrations in all countries in the first stages of the

---

181. The problem of substitution or fungibility of foreign aid refers to the possible negative impact of aid on other internal investments made by receiving countries. To the extent that these countries receive foreign aid, they can redirect at least partially some public funds (those funds that would have been spent in projects financed without ODA) to other sectors such as defence. Rahman, RD. and Andreu, JM. (2002/a: 67), book mentioned above.

development process[182]. We truly believe that governments of developing countries should put more emphasis on the correction of these problems; nevertheless this should not be a strong argument for *sine die* arresting the development process of the poorest countries.

As experienced by European countries in the last two decades, the deficiencies of the administration of the welfare state (to some extent corrupted) have been corrected, instead of being scrapped. This has occurred because the Europeans have wisely valued the importance of this system as a social stabiliser, over the evidence of nasty intra-system corruption and other de-stimulant failures. Likewise we do believe that although far from perfection, but probably on the road to good governance, administrations of developing countries should receive a temporal margin of confidence for correcting these problems in a context of UN regional supervision. Under our proposed scheme of significant public foreign finance reception, there will be some strong stimuli to limit corruption.

Concerning the second argument to limit current ODA, we have to emphasise that although private foreign sector could render some services in the field of infrastructure, energy, education or health, it is undeniable that the leading role in these activities should be played by the public sector. In particular since in general these activities cannot be profit-based as they are essential to meet necessities of the poor. Observe that the Western countries also implemented a similar strategy while realising their development process. Therefore we consider that if in the past the private sector in western countries was not involved in the production of public or merit goods, to hasty encourage its involvement in LDC is a misconception.

In relation to the alleged lack of absorption capacity of LDC, we have to state that this stance is quite irrelevant. The invoked arguments that "the absence of certain factors of production" such as skilled labour, or the existence of institutional problems, or the "endurance of inconvenient social and political organisation" may

---

182. Let us remember that underdevelopment has been historically linked with public controls and scant liberty in the markets, in particular the external one. These traits, connected with the low wages of civil servants has normally been conducive to public corruption.

hamper the implementation of development programmes in infrastructure, education and so on, seems to be a simple pretext. If Western countries give priority, as they should, towards promoting development, the focus should change from costs to the volume of devoted funds and the reorganisation of the transfer mechanisms of foreign public funds, which we shall describe below.

Finally we do recognise fungibility as a problem. Nevertheless, it is also possible to implement conditions for public transfers, once the system of transfers is reorganised and its volume increased. These conditions, as we will see, should contribute to limit the relevance of this problem of substitution or fungibility.

Summing up, there may be some problems that currently restrain the effectiveness of ODA. Notwithstanding that, we do believe that the basic reasons for its ineffectiveness have been its scant volume, its irrational distribution and its fragmentation. These are reasons that provoke lack of stimuli at the receiving end, thus avoiding surpassing the other above-mentioned sources of criticism.

6.4. A new approach for public transfers to bridge the gap

With the remarkable exceptions of the Marshall Plan which began in 1945, and the big push in civil and military aid given by US to a few selected countries in the "frontiers of communism" (South Korea, Taiwan), foreign aid has not been significantly effective in the last 50 years. Since the real and relative flows of foreign aid have dwindled in the last decade, and its geographical and per capita distribution remained highly disorganised and fragmented, we have to conclude that the current approach in development co-operation is in need of a fundamental change. In particular, if rich countries seriously want to bridge the gap, as an intermediate target to achieve peace and human security in the long term.

At the change of the millennium, an international call for a new approach gathered momentum, resulting in the establishing of the so-called UN millennium goals. The entire international community, including the Bretton Woods institutions accepted these goals set by the General Assembly of the UN. The most outstanding objective being the intention of halving the number of people under the poverty line by 2015. In our view this millennium goal, although positive is clearly insufficient to bridge the gap, which is the key economic target for reaching peace and prosperity for all.

On the wake of this, a UN panel lead by Dr. Zedillo[183] was installed to recommend a strategy for the mobilisation of resources required to fulfil the commitments on poverty and development, enshrined in the UN Millennium Declaration. In June 2001 the report of the Zedillo panel was presented to the General Assembly. It was a positive contribution to the financing of the development process, with the bold recognition that the challenges of the current process of globalisation cannot adequately be addressed by a system that was largely designed for the world of 50 years ago. For the first time a strong effort to achieve some international merit goods (basically education and health for all) was put on the table, together with a proposal for doubling the existing ODA up to 0.5% of the GDP of donors, as well as for reorganising the specialised agencies.

After the shock of September 11, a growing number of leading politicians started paying attention to the possible relation between poverty and exclusion to international terrorism. Centred in this reaction was a call for a concerted and urgent effort of the international community to fight against poverty as a basic way of addressing the breeding ground of terrorism. However, the Zedillo report recommendations of pushing up the ODA budget were not supported in March 2002 in Monterrey, at the UN conference on "Financing for Development".

It is clear that the hegemonic power was then much more confident in its military might for crunching terrorism than in looking for ways towards bridging the economic gap. With oblivion of the complementary action of investing in human development (health, education, infrastructure) in order to reduce hatred and other expressions of deprivation, an explicit choice was made for armed (pre-emptive) struggle against the so-called "axis of evil" countries[184].

In the aftermath of September 11, the scope of the suggestions of the Zedillo panel appeared to be limited, and the aesthetic millennium targets became clearly insufficient to quickly change the

---

183. Ernesto Zedillo was President of the Republic of Mexico in the 90s.

184. Note that the countries included in the "axis of evil" have no clear common denominator.

mood. The reactions in poorer parts of the world suggest that it is not only a matter of halving the number of people under the poverty line, but more a problem of bridging the gap at a high speed. This, added to the huge deficiencies of the current ODA, has inclined us to propose a boosting, pooling and reshuffling of the public international transfers to poorest countries, in the context of given targets for correcting part of the economic gap they are suffering.

6.5. A more ambitious target for bridging the gap

In our view, bridging the gap and the realisation of the main international public goods in a reasonable period of time, will require much more than doubling the existing squalid aid budget or the reestablishment of an outdated 0.7%[185] of GDP. Note that this figure was devised in an age when the donor countries had an aggregate real GDP of around half the current one. Instead of these figures we suggest a world-wide reorientation of public transfers of funds up to a figure of 2% of the GDP of donor countries. Observe that hereafter the words "aid" or "assistance" will not be mentioned in our proposal, simply because they are pejorative, implying a notion of charity and palliative action. Such a notion is completely alien to our proposal, which is directed towards significantly increasing investments in physical and human capital in LDC, as an intermediate target to achieve international public goods in a reasonable period of time.

Our plan for massive multilateral public transfers will change necessarily in the medium-long term into a win-win strategy, as it happened in Western Europe in the post Second World War era with the regional planning and the construction of the welfare state. In Europe, this development of massive transfers from rich to poor, be these persons or regions, enabled to overcome prior social tensions conducive to political and violent conflict escalation.

---

185. Note that if public foreign transfers (one of the sources of received foreign savings) are devoted to increase domestic investment, the growth rate of the recipient country will step up. This change in the growth rate will not be attained at random, as there are technical relations between effective growth rate, and the size of the domestic investments and the received foreign transfers. Consequently, if a target for the economic growth of LDC is proclaimed by rich countries, once the domestic savings of LDC are known, the volume of public foreign transfers to be provided by rich countries will result in an explicit percentage of their GDP.

In our plan, net-payer countries would globally transfer 2% of their GDP to a new UN institution (UNICO), in order that this institution be able to transfer multilateral grants[186] (not loans) to recipients for financing infrastructure, health and education, at a national and regional level. Since the current amount of contributions is now situated at around 0,23% of their GDP, it would be necessary to establish a phasing period of 5-7 years to reach the planned figure of 2%. Additionally we have to stress that the mentioned UN fund (UNICO) will work with a totally new approach of distribution, programming and monitoring based on ownership, regional co-operation, and regional planning at the receiving end.

6.5.1. *The rationality of the 2%*

At first reading and for several reasons many readers could consider this 2% figure to be nothing less than a joke. First of all because it would increase the current ODA budget by 8 times at a moment when the political trend in the West is precisely the opposite, which being minimising public expenditure[187]. Secondly because in the 90s ODA as part of foreign financing has been greatly surpassed by FDI, and consequently poor countries are expected to make all efforts in order to attract this huge source of foreign savings instead of looking for international public funds. Thirdly because an 8-fold increase of ODA would multiply the presumed problem of "absorption capacity". And finally because this relevant transfer of 2% rich countries GDP towards LDC could provoke macroeconomic problems (the so-called "transfer problem"), thus reducing further growth rates in donor countries.

Against these arguments we could say that the quantitative surpassing of ODA by FDI in the 90s was more a matter of orientation of the applied economic model in the West, than a proof

---

186. Note that our proposal for changing loans into grants made in March 2002, vide Rahman, R.D. and Andreu, J.M. (2002a: 86) has also recently been considered as positive by Gordon Brown in his Plan directed to IMF, mentioned lines above.

187. This may be the reason why the EU donors in Monterrey agreed to increase their ODA from the current 0.23% to a mere 0.30% after in-depth debates, while US promised grudgingly to increase their contribution up to 0.2% over a period of 5 years starting in 2004. A clear proof that the governments of these countries do not believe in the effectiveness of ODA to promote development, or otherwise that bridging the gap is not their priority at all.

of general superior efficiency of FDI for promoting development (remember the sequencing issue). Note additionally that this FDI at the end of the day only follows the private criteria of investments, thus logically ignoring poor countries where profit expectations are low. Experience has proved that the poorest countries practically do not receive any external flows but an extremely scant and disorganised ODA.

Indeed these countries, if they are short of infrastructure, energy and adequate human resources, will lack an absorption capacity for FDI, while in our view, they have an extremely high absorption capacity in human capital development (health and education) and basic infrastructure. Note that in many cases the financing of these activities could only be increased by resorting to higher international public transfers[188]. On the other hand, the difference in the budget between developed and developing countries in items such as infrastructure, health and education is so high that it may give sufficient margins for the mentioned 2% GDP absorption.

Concerning other (macroeconomic) aspects of the mentioned magnitude of the 2% of GDP to be pooled in UNICO for its transfer to LDC, we have to say that this amount has a complete guarantee for financial recycling. First of all because this 2% will be subject to a phasing period that will timely ease any recycling problems. On the other hand, let us remember that even after the two-oil crisis in the 70s, the international financial system was able to annually recycle up to 4% of the oil-consumers GDP, despite the limited import capacity of oil-producers. However in the case of the transfer of the above mentioned 2%, the recipients will voluntary buy (import) in a direct or indirect way from the rich countries a significant share of this 2%, reason why the international financial system will not be exposed to major risks.

Besides, within 5 to 7 years after starting the implementation of the plan, poverty in LDC would decline at a far more progressive rate as compared to the past decades, and the consumption growth rate of the citizens in net-paying countries would have recovered the past trend. Note that this consumption will not undergo any reduction of

---

188. Also Gordon Brown has recognised in his recent proposal to IMF that this is the correct sequencing for the external financing of development.

its absolute value at any moment due to the phasing of implementation and the expected growth of the GDP of rich countries.

6.5.2. *Implications of increased international public transfers up to 2%*

Although the above mentioned figure of 2% of the GDP for contribution to the UNICO may come as a surprise, this figure was recommended many years ago by the first Nobel-prize winner Jan Tinbergen[189] and by other institutions. But the most important principle underlying this 2% is that, according to the above described optimum sequencing for financing required for the development of poorest countries, this figure would be extremely useful in order to rationally shorten the period for bridging the gap. Doubtless, a reduced period of catching up will change the current trend of a boost in conflicts and the related deterioration in human security in the world. Finally one should recognise that this 2 % transfer will generate an additional increase in international trade, while at the same time rich countries will obtain lateral gains in the form of, for instance, significant reduction of illegal immigration and bogus asylum seeking.

As mentioned above, the recent spread of new forms of terrorism have several causes in which poverty, backwardness and the growing gap, far from being negligible, seems to be the core problem. Prolonging the Western non-consideration of these circumstances, or continuing the "error of sequencing" in bridging the gap, could drive the entire world into a situation of uncertainty. This situation would not only deter general prosperity but would also increase the insecurity at every level, national and individual, in many countries.

We believe that in the new tempo of history, a fourfold rise in the per capita GDP[190] of the least developed countries (low-income and middle-low income countries) in the next 25 years, which would shorten the gap within one generation, would be desirable. Consequently, a meaningful increase in the international public transfers up to 2% seems a reasonable target for the reduction of

---

189. Brandsma *et al.* (1996: 20). Jan Pronk. Scheffers, Amsterdam.

190. This per capita GDP has been reckoned in terms of exchange rates.

contemporary political threats, and consistent with an effective decrease of the current international economic gap.

6.5.3. *The economic scope of our proposals in comparison with others*

First of all, we have to say that an annual flow of 2% of the GDP of "high income" countries (in the terminology of the World Bank), would mean an increase of the international public transfers up to 460 billion US dollars. To give a better idea of its magnitude, these 460 billion US dollars is almost similar to the annual GDP in US dollars of countries like India or Mexico (in 2000).

If we establish as an aim the convenience of directing all future international public transfers to low-income and lower-middle-income developing countries (in the terminology of the World Bank), the above-mentioned 460 billion US dollars would inject in these LDC foreign savings to the tune of 13% of their own GDP. This injection could serve *ceteris paribus* to additionally boost their rhythms of per capita growth by 3.75%. An additional impulse that could make the average growth rate of the per capita GDP of this mixed group of countries reaches 6%. Or more if the problem of the population growth is progressively softened, and the pending problems of accessibility to developed markets are improved in the context of WTO.

Nevertheless, this very appreciable growth rate of 6% in per capita terms for the considered developing countries (equivalent to more than 8% increase of real GDP) will neither produce miracles nor dramatic changes in the short run, because it will only double the per capita income every 12 years. This means that the per capita GDP of this group of countries, placed currently as an average of 775 US dollars[191], will only equal the figure of 1550 US dollars in the year 2017 (after phasing considered) and that of 3100 in 2029. The above mentioned growth rates could significantly reduce, although step by step, the current growing economic gap, thus contributing to alleviate poverty and conflict, and enabling the attainment of international public goods.

---

191. This figure of 775 US dollars has been calculated in terms of exchange rates and not in PPP terms.

It is true that an annual increase of the international public transfers by 0.5% of GDP of rich countries, as defended by Gordon Brown, Kofi Anan and James Wolfensohn, would double the current squalid budget. However, with this budget a fourfold increase in the per capita GDP of the mentioned LDC would only be reached in a time-span of 46 years[192]. Too long a period to create enough hope to defuse the causes of current unrest and conflicts, while an increase up to 2%, would halve the time-span to 24 years[193]. Even worse, as the rest of the rich countries would continue growing, we consider that the 0.5% figure of GDP transfers will likely be insufficient to significantly bridge the gap.

6.6. UNICO as a new instrument for international public transfers

As many instruments and institutions born in the wake of the Second World War, the current institutions and instruments for financing development seem to be obsolete. In our view it is high time to implement a well-planned and efficient reform of the current international public transfers (non-system), justified on the similar grounds as that of the construction of the welfare state in Western countries, mainly in the golden age of capitalism. In this context of promotion of global welfare, our proposed 2% budget for co-operation should take the form of grants (not loans)[194].

The difference between our approach and the current non targeted and fragmented one, is that we consider the future (increased) transfers as an investment for reaching global welfare, from which Western countries could also draw significant profits in terms of increased

---

192. This additional increase of international public transfers could only enable an additional increase of 0.9% in the per capita income of these countries. This would mean that the per capita income of these countries would grow in the future at a rhythm of around 3.1%, a growth rate that would allow doubling their per capita income in 23 years, or quadrupling it in 46 years (3100 dollars of per capita income).

193. According to the new tempo of history, we have assumed that adults of the poorest countries would accept, in exchange for their effort, a better future for their children, not a better future for their grand children, whom they may never get to know.

194. Formally, there is no difference between the financial transfers from one national government to poorer regions of the same country, and the transfer of funds to other countries, when the favourable spill-over effects received by the countries which paid the transfers compensate its efforts (human security and peace).

exports, certainty in business, and increased security. These were precisely the issues, which were financed and thereby attained internally by the EU countries in the age of construction of their welfare state.

Conversely, the underlying thought of the Washington Consensus is just that of a moderate increase in the volume of soft loans and a hypothetical massive FDI directed towards LDC, because in their view there should be a strong prevalence of the private sector. A wrong purported substitution of the public sector in initial stages of development, based on the ignorance of correct sequencing, as history has proven.

6.6.1. *Main traits of the new UN instrument*

The best institutional framework for boosting, pooling, and reshuffling the financing for development should be the UN. Note however that the current UN has significant defects in its organisation and financing, as we have depicted in the lines above, and it is in need of structural reforms. Particularly since this institution has to control the 2 % fund for development financing.

Taken for granted that any modification of the current Charter of the UN will need the approval of all the 5 permanent members of the Security Council, we believe that consensus for such a modification will not be easy due to vested interest of (some) permanent members. In any case a new UN Charter will have to be devised. It is possible that some countries initially might not want to sign the new Charter since a new UN would imply higher funding obligations for them[195] and less power. Nevertheless as recent history has proven, we are convinced that at the end of the day almost everyone will opt for inclusion. This is because to remain outside global management will have severe political consequences and enormous economic costs[196]. In

---

195. As mentioned before, parallel to the additional economic burdens on the rich countries, they will also be the most beneficial of the new global economic environment created by the new international political framework. We are once again referring here to the experience of the general advantages, even for the rich, stemming from the creation and financing of welfare states in Europe, which demonstrated that the mechanism of taxing-subsidising is not a zero-game.

196. This is clearly illustrated by the case of the occupation of Iraq by the US and allies. After easily gaining the war, they have requested the help (troops) of other countries to stabilise the situation, because they are economically and politically not capable of sustaining the occupation by themselves.

this context the setting up of UNICO (UN International Co-operation Organisation) would be a natural derivative.

Entering into details we have to say that the policy aim of the UNICO is basically the achievement of intermediate targets, focussing on economic development of LDC in order to reach the already mentioned international public goods. For the operations many of the current UN specialised agencies, including World Bank, would merge under UNICO, and its new budget would be spent solely in grants.

The UNICO structure would consist of a central headquarter and several sub-regional UNICO bodies, the REUNICOs, in which governments of LDC in the region would participate. These REUNICOs could be organised by renewal and mergers of current regional UN associations.

6.6.2. *Expected outcomes of the UNICO system*

UNICO would allocate a budget per REUNICO on a biennial basis. The global budget of UNICO (equivalent to the total of all REUNICO budgets) should be distributed among candidate countries according to a certain "polynomial formula" for funding. The distribution would depend, among other variables, on the per capita GDP of every country, its degree of indebtedness, its military spending, its public deficit, its degree of internal saving, its internal distribution of income, its accessibility to external private funds, etc.

Accordingly, the volume of funding by every REUNICO would be the addition of the reckoned transfers to every country of the region, which would be related to some of the above-mentioned variables, thus creating a stimuli to solve problems of governance, fungibility, and regional conflicts. In order to finance joint sub-regional projects (in the interest of two or more countries) a significant percentage, f.i. 20%, of total funding of the region would be kept at REUNICO's disposal. The global funding from UNICO would depend on the timely progressive transfers to UNICO carried out by net-paying rich countries.

To guarantee ownership and efficiency among LDC, each REUNICO would propose biennial development priorities, in order to apply the appraisal criteria formulated by UNICO. After approval by UNICO, the funding could start working. In every REUNICO, independent chairs would be appointed by UNICO. These chairpersons should come from other regions and should be internationally renowned.

Note that in order to qualify for participation in REUNICO, the LDC of the region will have to solve both internal violent conflicts and conflicts with neighbouring countries, which would trigger conflict resolution in the region and increase regional co-operation in economic and political matters. This multilateral treatment of transfers and previous qualifications are circumstances completely alien to the current non-system, which has no capabilities to stimulate internal and external conflict resolution.

Concerning the current foreign indebtedness of poor countries (Severely Indebted Countries or SIC), the UNICO system will allow the automatic cancellation or rescheduling of the outstanding debts of SIC, if they qualify for participation in UNICO. The huge budget of the UNICO system will allow the recipients to choose the rescheduling period, leaving the concerned SIC with enough room for selection of more project financing and less debt cancellation or vice-versa.

Last but not the least, UNICO would stimulate the devolution of decision-making and ownership to the recipients at the level of REUNICOs, given the fact that REUNICOs will have the last say in putting priorities in accordance with the general criteria set by UNICO.

6.7. The commitment to sustainability

Along this essay we have devised a strategy to facilitate poverty alleviation and to bridge the economic gap, in order to defuse the negative impacts of extreme international economic inequalities on peace and human security. One essential piece of this strategy is the acceleration of the growth rate of LDC. However, this stepping up of economic progress of LDC will have to be consistent with the maintenance of the environment assets of the involved countries (and with those of the net-payers) and with the adequate management of their non-renewable resources. This means that the growth acceleration should not additionally degrade the quality of available air, water, soil, landscape, etc., or otherwise it should generate a greater volume of *ad hoc* goods and services to offset some (although) acceptable environmental degradation. If not the registered increase of the speed of economic growth would to some extent be fictitious[197].

The problem of the environment is not only a matter of poor countries, but also of the richest ones. Evidence shows that the worst perpetrators of environmental destruction in the world are the billion richest on the one hand, and the billion poorest people on the other[198]. The rich because of their consumerism, in particular in relation with their lavish energy consumption, and the poor because of their pressing survival needs, mainly stemming from poverty and high fertility rates, combined with chaotic urbanisation.

The pressing needs force the rural poor in LDC to overuse the resources at their disposal, progressively clearing the forest to meet their food and fuel needs, which is conducive to deforestation, desertification, and to soil degradation.

In the urban areas of developing countries, the supply of public services cannot match the enormous increase of rural migrants that dwell in overcrowded shantytowns and slums. Basic infrastructure, adequate shelter, distribution of energy, and safe water and sanitation are in enormous deficit in poor countries. This is conducive to individual and inefficient solutions by the poor who use wood as fuel, boil unsafe water, pollute soil and rivers etc. And this while in these countries the rich and middle class citizens, who hardly pay direct taxes, often have access to subsidised electricity and water.

In order to correct these micro-environmental problems, poor countries should improve the definition of property rights (in particular to solve the problem of communal goods), establish a correct pricing for improving the allocation of resources, and initiate the correction of the negative externalities.

---

197. We could here remember the example of Indonesia. After deep research some analysts reached the conclusion that half of the growth rate registered in the 70s, was not sustainable, since in the System of National Accounts of those days the degradation of environment resources were not detracted from the GDP. Repetto, R. (1987) "Natural resources accounting for Indonesia". Washington D.C. World Resources Institute, May. Vide also the new system of macro-accountancy, as explained by World Bank (2003) in its "World Development Indicators.

198. Todaro, M. and Smith, S. (2003: 466), book already mentioned.

The latter could be corrected by means of imposing taxes or establishing quantitative limits to emissions. And all this in the context of new fiscal systems less inclined towards indirect taxes.

6.7.1. *Earth warming, polluters, and pretexts*

Letting aside national environmental problems, whose solutions are in delay in most LDC, we will now look into the environment at a global level, focussing on the interrelated issues of rain forest destruction, greenhouse gases, and global warming. In relation to the issue of greenhouse gases (CO_2) in the atmosphere it is possible to distinguish two broad groups of causal activities: the industrial production with around 3/4 of emissions, and the rest of activities. Note that developing countries with roughly 4/5 of the global population, produce less than 1/3 of industrial emissions (only 1/5 if we exclude China).

This means that the higher the per capita income in Western countries, the higher the industrial per capita emissions of CO_2. The case of the US is a somewhat overdone paradigm of the former proposition. The level of per capita emissions of the US is well over the average in Europe, 19 times the average in Africa and even 23 times higher than the average in India. Although developing countries issue a small proportion of industrial CO_2, they generate practically all the non-industrial greenhouse gases (fuel-wood, burning vegetation to clear plots etc.). Note that clearing of forests due to pressing needs for food, or overexploitation of tropical rain forests, reduce the capacity of green masses to regenerate the atmosphere.

Although from a scientific point of view the positive correlation between emissions of CO_2, mainly generated by industrialised countries, and earth-warming has not been completely determined, it does point out that global warming and climate change started some 200 years ago, since the inception of the industrial revolution. However this earth warming has only become perceivable in the last 3 decades.

To the extent that maintaining non-exploited rain forests in the world (mainly based in developing countries) would help to offset CO_2 emissions, most industrial countries are constantly putting pressure on LDC to preserve their forests despite the fact that the rich countries are the main macro-polluters. Note that at the same time these rich countries refuse to significantly pay for the actions realised to counter economic exploitation of rain forests, thus behaving as free riders.

In this case, one may follow once again the asymmetric behaviour of rich countries on issues related to developing countries. Depending on whether matters are seen as pure internal business, Western countries (including the US) apply the recipes of the neo-classical model concerning externalities, by means of devising sophisticated mechanisms as those of tradable emission permits, thus somewhat applying the principle of "those who pollute should pay".

As it happens in many other fields of economic policy, as f.i. in free movements of people and workers, in the Western countries what is true inside is not valid outside, and therefore they do not pay for global pollution, using manifold pretexts. To make matters worse, some prominent countries, as the US and China, which are the two main CO_2 polluters in the world have still not ratified the Kyoto treaty on climate change[199].

6.7.2. *Global agreements but little implementation*

Although the first global summit on sustainable development in Rio de Janeiro (1992) produced an impressive Agenda 21, in the second Summit in Johannesburg, 10 years later, it became clear that the implementation of the Rio agenda was very far from being accomplished. This Agenda 21 included a wide scale of issues such as poverty alleviation; provision of clean water and sanitation; reduction of soil erosion; family planning and education; protection of habitat and bio-diversity; and research and development of non-carbon energy alternatives to respond to earth warming etc.

In relation to the Agenda 21 and its poor development, we have to say that most of the countries, be these rich or poor have limited themselves to some internal pro-environment activities. However scant steps were taken by different countries in relation to macro-

---

199. The Kyoto treaty of 1997 deals with the reduction in 2010 of greenhouse gases issued by western countries to their pre-levels of 1990. At the establishment of the treaty developing countries refused to commit any action from their side, awaiting the actions of the rich countries.

issues such as climate change, bio-diversity, the protection of tropical rain forest, and so on.

It is a matter of fact that although poverty has been considered generally as one of the major causes of further environmental degradation, in the past decade, the fight against poverty has been practically left to the forces of a freer market devised in a selective way. Consequently, the speed of poverty reduction has been irksome slow.

Once again the schedule of the political process in democratic countries has not matched with the necessary long-term and steady actions to be implemented in issues such as poverty alleviation and environmental protection. Given the fact that poverty alleviation is an urgent problem to be solved, we are convinced that for achieving real progress, macro-level initiatives for sustainable development and bridging the gap should be taken, financed and enforced by the UN in the context of a more ambitious policy.

Concerning the implementation of these UN macro-level initiatives to improve the global environment, our proposal of 2% GDP transfers could be an optimal instrument to introduce an ad hoc rational mechanism of subsidies and taxes. This instrument should be capable of rewarding rich or poor countries that surpass the temporal targets of UN designed calendars for environmental protection, or to penalise these rich or poor countries when they do not meet the proposed time frame. This would mean that pro-environment rich countries would pay less than 2%, and pro-environment LDC would receive more funding from UNICO.

6.8. A new approach on conflict management

The spectre of international conflicts has changed considerably over the last decades. Next to the more traditional interstate wars in which the protection of national territory and political sovereignty were the main aims, intra-state conflicts and wars against international terrorism, are somewhat new types of conflicts.

Even though intrastate conflicts (civil wars) comprised the majority of violent conflicts since the Second World War, they have received international attention only after the end of the Cold War. Till then this category of conflict was overshadowed by superpower rivalry, often supporting either side of the intrastate conflicts.

There are salient differences between the classic interstate war fought between the armies of two or more states (formally restricted by international law), and intrastate conflict. The latter is less restricted in terms of civilian rights, has often no declared beginning and no clear end, makes no distinction between civilians and military, and is generally of a protracted nature. During the course of intrastate conflict, the issues and causes, parties and modalities may change. It is often difficult to identify the parties involved and their leadership, and it is therefore, not easy to find good interlocutors to discuss resolution.

International terrorist attacks are not a new phenomenon in the world, but after September 11, with the start of the so-called International War against terrorism, lead by the US, this problem is more at the forefront. There are again salient differences between the classical interstate war and the war against terrorism, since in the latter case neither the battlefield or the combatants are identifiable.

For the two anti-terrorist wars recently fought by the US and its allies, the hegemonic power surprisingly defined the contour of the battlefield, in such a way that the US could conveniently fight a traditional interstate war and win.

Nevertheless some terrorist leaders seemed to have survived the wars while the population in these two countries have unduly suffered a collective punishment and awaits an almost *sine die* reconstruction.

Countries suspected of providing shelter to terrorist groups, or of producing WMD or of supplying them to these groups, were included in the list of countries defined as the so-called Axis of Evil. This list is open-ended and the inclusion in such a list is seemingly used by the hegemonic power as a political weapon. Hence the countries included in the list may change into possible targets for interstate wars and occupation.

One could wonder if these inadequate and ad hoc interstate wars have resulted in the elimination of terrorist groups. In both cases the US and its allies have brought destruction and chaos in these countries, till now without meaningful improvement in the life of the average citizens. If things do not improve in due time the image of the US and its allies in the Muslim world will further deteriorate.

This may lead to strengthened feelings of hatred, which again is a good breeding ground for terrorism, thus creating a vicious circle.

6.8.1. *New types of conflicts in need of new approaches*

In terms of conflict management of intrastate war and war against terrorism, it is clear that the existing multilateral political and legal framework (United Nations and Security Council) is inadequate. On the other hand, in this case a bilateral approach is no substitute due to the possible lack of ethical and moral guidance not only on the side of the combatants but also on the side of bilateral mediating parties, who at times meet their own interests. Hence our call for a new international infrastructure and treaties for conflict management of intrastate wars and wars against terrorism, in the context of a renewed UN, as proposed in the lines above.

Let us remember that the history of the UN peacekeeping has been a chronicle of quite a number of failures[200] often followed by corrective bilateral armed interventions. These failures obey to the lack of equilibrium among the individual powers of the different nations in the UN, and the lack of interest of the powerful in democratising the organisation that consequently would dilute their own power.

The small budget of the UN, including the regular one and that for peacekeeping, is an indicator of the scant multilateral capabilities put together by the international society to deal with such an important issue as conflict resolution and its consequences in terms of huge loss of innocent lives. If we add to this the veto rights of the five permanent members and their comparative defence supremacy, a framework prone to bilateral interventions and multilateral breakdown is a necessary result.

Consequently, if we want to reverse the disappointing steps taken by the UN in recent conflicts, it is necessary to restructure the UN capabilities on conflict management, including the option for UN lead armed intervention, and to significantly multiply its budget. Only these changes could transform the UN in an operational

---

200. One could here remember the cases of Kashmir, Palestine, Libanon, Congo, Somalia, Bosnia, Rwanda, and Sierra Leone. Vide Mingst, K. and Karrns, M. (2000: 78), book already mentioned.

multilateral agency for early warning, conflict management, peacemaking, peacekeeping, and generalised arms control and disarmament activities.

Against the background of the current impossibility of armed intervention by the UN with its forces, while at the same time intrastate wars have become more destructive, bilateral interventionism is forceful but limited in results if there are not enough direct economic interests at stake. In this regard the position of the permanent members of the Security Council, which pathetically ignore the ongoing intrastate wars in poorer regions of the planet, is absolutely shocking.

Concerning international terrorism, the UN should identify the main sources of it, the hosting states, and devise a mixed strategy of carrots and sticks instead of indiscriminate punishment of innocent citizens in the rogue states as recently practised. Diplomatic mediation concerning interaction with terrorist groups should not be forgotten or condemned in advance, irrespective of their final ends, but promoted. It is important to know the ultimate reasons for terrorist actions.

As shown in Chapter 3, some countries hosting terrorists appear to be among the countries with the highest per capita income disparity and lower per capita GDP in relation to per capita income of rich countries. This is something to be urgently corrected as proposed in this essay, by setting up UNICO and the speedy implementation of the proposed policies concerning international public transfers.

7

Findings, Conclusions and Recommendations

A Programme for Global Stability and Institutional Reform

Along the previous chapters we have reviewed the current state of political instability and economic uncertainty in the world. In our view these negative traits have been created basically by longstanding unresolved regional conflicts, unfair treatment towards developing countries in developing financing and in international economic and political negotiations, and last but not the least by an imprudent neglect of the growing economic gap.

Believing that economic backwardness is a fertile breeding ground for violent conflict and terrorism, we have firstly focused on the recent evolution of mainstream economic philosophy, with special reference to the current western interpretation of the neo-classical model. The analysis of this particular interpretation has also been useful in order to explain the ground of constant complains and disappointment of LDC and the rest of the developing countries.

To value the complaints of developing countries more accurately, we have analysed the economic evolution and compared the standards of living in the different regions of the world in the past two centuries, with a special reference being made to the Muslim-Arab world. Because of its special importance for future developments, we have also considered the growing US-EU economic gap. We have also deemed the insufficient policies of international economic institutions, the main supporters of the current economic doctrine and, to some extent, the responsible bodies for the evolution of economic differentials and the growing gap in the last three decades.

After these considerations we have entered into the analysis of the evolution of underlying political philosophy, today centred in a sort of Darwinism mixed with consumerism and short-termism. In this political context we have also discussed the trade off between efficiency and equity in the short and long term. From a historical perspective, we have also analysed the evolution of international power sharing since 1945, explaining the changes in the power correlation starting from mid 80s, and the possible inconveniences caused by the appearance of a new hegemonic power.

Before entering into the presentation of our programme for global stability and institutional reform, we have discussed some historical precedents, which could enlighten rich countries on possible future reactions of poorest countries, and some groups of individuals. We have also reviewed the historical case of informed (European) societies in connection with growing economic gaps among social classes, and we have assumed that this experience is now internationally applicable to the current growing economic unbalances.

In order to correct the *huge* and *negative* economic and political trends suffered by LDC, we have outlined a programme directed towards financing the development of the poorest countries, and improving their access to the markets of rich countries for bridging the current growing economic gap. We have also explained that a new system of boosted, pooled and reorganised development financing should be multilateral and organised under the aegis of the UN.

Taking into consideration that the current organisation of the UN, as described in its Charter, is refractory towards a more democratic representation, is inefficient in its working and lacks due financing, we have outlined a primary roadmap for its reform. We have also made some considerations in relation with sustainable development, given the cross-border and relevant spill-over effects of the emissions to the environment. Finally, we have introduced some tentative ideas on effective conflict resolution.

7.1. Main findings and data for analysis

There is no doubt that since September 11, the world has entered into a new stage of political history. Note however that the international power structure had already started to change in the 80s, when the Soviet Union began to crumble.

The disintegration of the USSR was basically a consequence of the incapability of its economy to continue supporting the arms race with the US, mixed with growing discontent of its citizens on the economic gap with the capitalist world, which was unveiled thanks to the ongoing Communications and IT revolution. After the fall of the Berlin Wall, the unexpected fast collapse of the East Block, and the patched policy practised by the US in the 90s, September 11 marked a watershed in the international political framework.

With disputable founded reasons, with a minimum of post-war planning, and in one case without multilateral support, US has attacked and defeated the regimes of two small countries (Afghanistan and Iraq), looking for quick fixes without finally getting what it initially purported. This powerful country has also defined a tentative list of countries (the so-called Axis of Evil) with assumed hosting of terrorist groups, or capability of using or trafficking in WMD. These listed countries may become targets of pre-emptive US military action, by-passing UN resolutions, if necessary.

Two main causes may explain this inconvenient global behaviour of the US. First of all the disappearance of the former countervailing power, that till the 80s and in some way, played a significant role as an international political stabiliser, deterring expansionist adventures of the other bloc. The disappearance of this countervailing power, without an emerging one to replace it, has left the world at the moods of a somewhat detached power. This hegemonic power if it is acting in a unilateral way may become risky, or at least counterproductive, as it occurs in economics with monopolies.

Secondly, we cannot overlook the fact that the US has continued its weapons development, placing the rest of the world in a second tier position from the point of view of defence capabilities. Thus, the US has become the only military super power, with proven destructive capacities, which may change into a serious global problem[201] if its leadership does not act linearly and with moral authority.

7.1.1. Possible reasons for growing international terrorism

Presenting a complete perspective of the changes taking place after September 11, we have looked into the possible reasons for growing international terrorism. We have found two main origins,

---

201. "The Economist" (2003). Greatest danger or greatest hope? 8th November.

one economic and the other political. The economic cause must have been the growing gap. We should not forget that in the era of the new liberalism (1973-1998), according to the definition and figures of Madisson (2001), the regional per capita GDP gap has at a global level increased from 13:1 to 19:1. Note that with the exception of the period 1950-1973, this growing disparity, far from being a-typical, has maintained the same trend since 1870. In those days of 1870, with the commencement of the era of "classical liberalism", the per capita GDP gap among regions of the world was only 5:1.

However, frustrations do not only derive from the economic front. They could also be found in the political field. Particularly among communities that, after bitter fighting and their cases being acknowledged by UN resolutions, have not received justice due to the related resolutions not being implemented, as for instance in the case of Palestine. This could be cited as a good example of the underlying political reasons conducive to international terrorism.

With reference to the Arab-Muslim world, Afghanistan is a paradigm of a dreadful combination of both factors. In 1998 the per capita GDP disparity in Afghanistan in comparison to the OECD countries reached an unbearable figure of 42.8:1. No wonder this comparatively harsh economic reality has enhanced a vengeance in the form of hard drugs cultivation and smuggling, and the hosting of terrorist organisations.

Since 1870 the growing economic gap has been the rule and its reduction the exception. Consequently the growing economic disparities in terms of per capita GDP experienced between rich and poor regions of the world in the last 3 decades, has not been accidental. In our view it has been a derivative of a specific wrong approach to the neo-classical model, interpreted in favour of the rich countries.

7.1.2. *On the working of the current mainstream economic approach*

After the practical disappearance of the socialist economic approach, as a consequence of its incapability to elucidate the reality and bear fruits, it is clear that the only operative model that explains acceptably the behaviour of economic agents is the neo-classical one. Notwithstanding that, due to the existence of market failures (monopolistic behaviour, externalities, public goods, insufficient or asymmetric information, etc.) public interventions have always been necessary. In this context, the morphology (direct or indirect) of public intervention, and its degree of involvement, that is to say its size, has for decades been a matter of discussions. Nonetheless the public sector grew continuously along the 20th century till the 70s at a global scale.

In the 80s, in the wake of the contributions of monetarists, new-neo-classicals, public-choice-theorists, and supply-siders, all of them criticising exaggerations practised by governments founded on strong interventionism and a primitive interpretation of Keynesian economics, applied economics turned in most of the countries to new but reversed exaggerations.

According to the new critics of interventionism and Keynesian economics, many activities were to be quickly liberalised and managed by the private sector, economies should be swiftly export-reoriented, and international movements of capital should be free. Last but not the least all the macroeconomic equillibria should also be fulfilled. In its new reorientation, mainstream economics supported and enhanced by the so-called Washington Consensus (WB, IMF and US Treasury) played a significant role. Along the 90s these institutions defined the "necessary conditions" for development of LDC and their catching up process.

Nevertheless, in our opinion this Washington Consensus doctrine has many loopholes. Firstly due to technical limitations or ignorance in advance of the different dynamic results of the applied neo-classical model, when the liberalisation process is undertaken at different speeds. And also in relation to the possible inconvenience of liberalising some markets while others, or just one, remains non-liberalised (so called "second best problem"). Secondly by the wrong definition of the "necessary conditions" for development. In our view many of these conditions considered as "necessary" by the Washington Consensus are neither necessary nor sufficient, as history of development has proven. And thirdly, due to the fact that the sequencing in liberalisation processes, at international level, has constantly followed the interests of the rich countries.

In this regard the asymmetry deployed in international negotiations is commonly shared among independent economists.

Note that the pressure put on developing countries by the rich in GATT rounds, has mainly been on the reduction of tariff and non-tariff barriers on their imports of industrial products coming from the West. In the mean time, US, EU, Japan, etc, have kept high barriers on imports of agricultural goods from developing countries.

More recently, in the days of the WTO, the implementation by rich countries of market accessibility for agricultural products and services coming from developing countries is in delay. At the same time these rich countries have continued pressing for widening the issues for negotiation with the so-called new (Singapore) issues. Regrettably once again the priorities put by the West are not impregnated by enlightened self-interest but rather by short-term considerations. Letting aside all this, the lack of concern in the main stream economic approach for the need of increasing international public transfers to promote the development of developing countries (mainly LDC) and for a freer movement of labour, continues.

7.1.3. *The future role of the EU in international politics*

Redirecting the focus on the international economic results in the last two decades, and comparing economic performance of the US and the EU during the said period, we have to certify that the EU has lost meaningful economic ground vis a vis US. This loss of ground could have significant repercussions in the formulation of international policies in the first decade of the 21st Century and will willy-nilly affect all countries.

There are several causes that explain the lesser growth rate of the EU productivity per worker in the last 20 years, in comparison with that of the US. Among them we could here refer to the domestic segmentation of some EU markets, the lack of competition in others, the absence of a clear shared code of conduct in economic action abroad, and finally, the much lesser number of worked hours per person. All these traits have placed the EU in a second tier economic position, and many of them have to be corrected as soon as possible.

Letting aside the long-term development of the EU-25 in the context of the new European Constitution, there is no doubt that the best way to introduce necessary corrections is by means of setting up a voluntary federation among the interested EU-12 countries. This federation would enable the federated countries to save up to 2% of their GDP, given the reachable economies of scale in some relevant public services to be merged (Defence, Foreign Representation, Finance, Borders Control, etc). The reorganisation of part of its administration, and its parallel financial saving, would allow the European Federation to reduce some taxes, to enhance international finance for bridging the gap, and supporting global environmental improvements, and perhaps undertake new internal public services. As a result, the European production machinery would improve and the EU would be able to gain clout in its international political involvement, thus enabling the EU to act as a constructive countervailing power, playing a more important role in conflict management.

One relevant aspect in the reformulation of a new international economic strategy, is the reconsideration of the "apparent existence" of a trade-off between efficiency and equity. For long, and especially nowadays, many authors and institutions have defended the idea that improving equity has enormous costs in terms of efficiency. However, history has supplied a lot of evidence confirming that this statement is wrong in the long term.

In effect, when we refer to the case of informed societies (blossoming thanks to the communication and IT revolution) across the world, we should deduce that sharp economic unevenness is politically untenable in the long term, as it happened within Europe in the first half of the 20th century. In Europe, the former social equilibrium (typical of rural societies) in which economic injustice and ignorance coexisted, broke down when people became conscious of the abuses they suffered. From this moment onwards, severe conflict surged and escalation started.

These violent conflicts have usually been long lasting (sometimes decades), or have for long generated uncertainty with loses for all. Note that the capacity for repression of the army or the police of liberal Western states was a priori much more "convincing" than the constant, and grey step by step initiatives of the Trade Unions. However, after decades of internal conflicts and two World Wars, some subsequent common sense appeared to defuse sharp internal conflicts forever, by means of creation of the Welfare State in Europe. Unfortunately, till now this welfare distribution pattern (which requires massive public transfers) has not been transplanted to development financing by Western countries.

7.2. Expectable reactions of Developing Countries

If we read the signs of time (articles in news papers in developing countries, interventions in multilateral institutions etc.) it becomes clear that the rather well informed citizens of LDC will not remain passive in a situation of economic and political exclusion. From the available data and applying common sense, we have depicted the following possibilities.

First of all, if rich countries continue with their traditional greedy pattern in trade negotiations or in their contribution to development financing, they could be confronted with a prospect of increasing illegal immigration and bogus asylum seeking (and as a derivative with more human trafficking). These would be individually adopted solutions against exclusion, but backed by the human right of the people to move geographically in order to earn a living by means of working. When Mafiosi arrange these movements however, human rights based initiatives turn into criminal activity.

In second place, long lasting feelings of hopeless frustration, rooted in indefinite and informed poverty, or exclusion, or in a mix of these humiliations, could be, as it has already happened, conducive to increased terrorism, in particular international terrorism. The latter is specially directed against citizens and assets of some rich countries, targeted by terrorists for being allegedly responsible for the political and economic impasse to which they are confined.

Letting aside the former reactions, based on initiatives of individuals or groups, one may also imagine some co-operative non-violent actions, undertaken by LDC or relevant developing countries. A movement towards additionally strengthening trade regionalism, in demerit of the multilateral approach, is already clearly underway. Although this is a movement against global welfare, the EU will not be in a position to complain, as this has for long been its game. The same although in a minor tone could be said about the US since the creation of the NAFTA. A regionalist game that, besides, is legal in the context of the WTO rules.

Western countries should not rule out the possibility that some relevant developing countries (f.i. China, India, Brazil), invoking specific principles of GATT, act in order to divert some important western flows of exports to the involved developing countries. These kinds of actions could be disruptive for western economies, thereby arresting or reversing their cyclical trajectory. Although in the near future these actions would possibly be less troublesome than some decisions made in the past by OPEC, this could significantly change in the next decades when the demand for certain goods is mainly made by Asia.

It is clear that negotiations are preferable over confrontation, except in the case that, in the opinion of one side, supported by facts, the other side does not offer any room of manoeuvring in order to improve the terms of trade. Remembering the history of trade unions and their actions as countervailing powers to reach competitive market positions concerning wages and working conditions, one could easily foresee eventual international economic skirmishes and trade-battles. These, *ceteris paribus*, could start taking place in the current decade, if they have not already started (Cancun failure).

If any variant of the above described wars become a reality or international terrorist actions continue, the world might then enter into a situation of sluggish development, stagnation or even something worse, induced by a long-lasting uncertainty about the future. However, to address this situation, it is clear that the western countries cannot opt for invading the other side, as it used to occur in colonial times. And if they do, the world would then reinitiate a dangerous process of colonialism, in which even the current UN would have no space to survive.

However in our view, the situation would not deteriorate to that extent without any reaction from some Western countries. It is possible that the first efficient reaction against unjust actions concerning LDC comes from Europe. To be successful this reaction should, in our view, include efforts for changing the current patterns of international trade and public foreign financing of LDC. Of course, the construction of a voluntary European Federation would be significantly helpful, due to the fact that the reachable "economies of integration" would allow it to pay for the required increased transfers for financing development without increasing taxes.

Consequently we do believe that in the context of the existence of an EU federation, the uncertainty generated by potential commercial wars could enter into a more eased stage.

7.3. A programme for global stability
and institutional reform

World stability cannot be achieved in a world with huge and ever increasing income disparities among different nations, or in a world radically unfair due to long-lasting and hopeless exclusion of many communities. Consequently, if we seriously want to improve the human environment of our planet, by making it more liveable in a *reasonable period of time*, we would urgently need to introduce a number of important innovations.

According to our judgement, any political action to be carried out in the future has to be multilateral, but the multilateral institutions available today are basically outdated and obsolete. Let us remember that they were established at the end of the Second World War, when the circumstances were radically different. The victors devised a UN at convenience, and the rest of the countries that were initially signing, less than 50, adjusted. The same happened with the Bretton Woods institutions (WB and IMF), and other initial offspring's of the UN, as GATT.

Note that in those days even those colonies that were on the verge of acquiring their independence, practically did not play any role in the inception of the UN and they remained mainly excluded from the international political process. Nevertheless, only three decades later, most of them had embodied the UN and claimed a more dynamic economic development. Unfortunately for them, at that time the "golden age" of capitalism had already ended and the multilateral institutions changed their discourse, adjusting it to the available (scant) amount of funds for development, while consecrating a new economic doctrine, an incomplete and biased version of neo-classicism.

In general we do not believe in military interventions in order to solve problems related with global instability. Conversely we consider civil actions as a priority to deal with the causes of the mentioned instability. Having said this, we think that it is absolutely essential to initiate a significant manoeuvre for bridging the economic gap and to guarantee sustainable development for contemporary and future generations at the earliest. This requires an urgent reorganisation of the UN, endowing it with more funds and more multilateral functions related to development financing and conflict resolution.

If the nations of the world, especially the rich countries, are not capable of solving these problems, the derivative will be the continuation of violent conflicts, terrorist attacks, more international criminal economic activities, more illegal immigration, and eventual economic or commercial second best actions with loses for all. Among these non-desirable actions we have already mentioned the increase in regional trade blocs, "import diversion" of relevant western exports, particularly from Europe, etc.

In order to avoid repetitions and without entering in extensive explanations, already given in the previous chapters, we will simply summarise the main reforms to be implemented in order to reach the essential international public goods (peace and security) to guarantee global stability. We are confident that with the below mentioned reforms the world can avoid a global economic stalemate and a gloomy social prospect that *ceteris paribus* could occur in the near future.

7.3.1. *Points for urgent action*

1. We are convinced that the moment of the truth has arrived. The world cannot continue depending on international institutions created in the second half of the 40s, since these have become extremely outdated and non-operative. While the ultimate goals of the UN remain being of great value for mankind, the organisation and decision-making processes are not only obsoletes but also restricted to any change from within. A striking example of its obsolescence is that the current hegemonic power, being the host country of the UN headquarters, can misuse its consular power to veto the composition of representatives of member countries, thus prejudicing the independence of the UN. Even more, the current location of the UN headquarters, which might have been appropriate at the time of the UN inception, today is economically inefficient. For these and other reasons we recommend that a new UN headquarter is placed in a functional city around the Mediterranean Sea.

2. A major aspect of reforming the decision-making process of the UN is the reformulation of its Security Council. Its current composition and privileges devised at the end of the Second World War are democratically unacceptable. Taking into account the principles of efficiency and representation, the number of member

countries could be widened up to 24, this being re-equilibrated in regional terms, while the status and veto right of the so-called permanent members (UK, France, Russia, China and the US) should be cancelled. This privilege is a clear anachronism, which is improper to the democracy that four of these five members state to defend.

3.   Since the necessary reform of the Security Council, among other conditions, would require the change of the UN Charter, and since the ruling UN Charter can only be changed with the full support of the 5 permanent members, reforming the UN from inside is highly unlikely. It seems more reasonable to open a new external constituting process, in which a new broader based Charter would be agreed upon. This Charter, besides changing the Security Council and streamlining the UN, should devise a new scheme of development financing that enables pooling, boosting and reorganising a massive public and multilateral transfer of funds during a generation for reaching international public goods and global sustainability.

4.   Although the principle of contribution according to the ability to pay should continue ruling for general assessed budget-contributions, we believe that the current pattern should be changed significantly. Allowing almost half of the UN members to pay altogether only 1% of the annual budget, while the 5 richest members together pay 2/3 of the bill, is a clear mistake in the distribution of the burden, which prejudices the administration and representation. By experience we can say that accepting non-contributing positions of almost a majority of the members of any club is conducive to lack of responsibility and squandering of resources. On the other hand those members, which pay much more than the rest tend to grab influence and snatch power. Similarly arrears in financing should not be allowed, they should rather be penalised with suspension or even expulsion, as it is an intolerable and unfair mechanism potentially usable to choke the UN working.

5.   In the past fifty years neither explicit nor consistent targets have been established by international economic institutions in order to correct the dangerous growing economic gap. A missed opportunity, particularly in the last decade, since reducing the gap is a necessary condition to reach peace, human security and world stability as explained in the previous chapters. To reduce the economic gap, the rich countries should count with two

complementary instruments. First, by increasing funds, pooling and reshuffling them for financing the development of LDC through a UN body (UNICO), in order to overcome the scant, disorganised and untargeted current ODA. And second, by changing the current purely short-term and consequently irrational behaviour of western countries in international economic negotiations (trade, labour, etc.).

6. After the commencement of the implementation of the massive transfers of funds to LDC by UNICO, and similarly to what has happened with the recent development of the international free mobility of capital, rich countries should initiate a more generous, although phased, policy of admission of migrant workers. These two actions, properly co-ordinated will surely be profitable for all sides in the long term (improvement of allocation of resources), and will deter illegal immigration and growing bogus asylum seeking, and as a result counter the Mafiosi organisations that control this inhuman trafficking.

7. To finance required domestic investments for catching up, LDC will have to resort to foreign financing since their domestic savings are often very scant. Due to the fact that private foreign funding in their different forms (basically FDI and Portfolio Investments) have systematically overlooked LDC, as proven by recent economic history, poor countries are left with no other option than to receive international public transfers till they can attract significant FDI. That is to say, till they can count with sufficient infrastructure, communications, and sufficient internal savings and human capital to become profitable for private investors.

8. We are convinced that the so-called "necessary conditions" for development and catching up as formulated by the Bretton Woods institutions (Washington Consensus), are neither necessary nor sufficient. Consequently, if LDC start or continue with the reforms as prescribed by the Washington Consensus, assuming that after doing so, foreign private capitals will automatically and abundantly flow to complement the insufficient domestic savings for catching up, many of them will result disappointed. They should remember that even inside the developed world, particularly in the EU countries and the US, some regions have been in need of additional massive public expenditures in infrastructure, health and education to converge with the rest. These massive transfers were necessary although these poor

regions counted with the same liberal conditions as the rest of the nation (including internal free movements of commodities and capital). Even more, inside these countries the free movement of people (internal migration) has been the main support for regional convergence in per capita GDP. Note that an international freer movement of people is by no means part of the" necessary conditions" of the Washington Consensus.

9. We are conscious that the current mainstream economics is refractory to the international public financing of development. In this regard a whole range of arguments have been put on the table to choke any serious initiative based on this mean of development financing. One of the most frequently mentioned is the lack of good governance in LDC, and the related problems such as corruption and non-accountability. The second, a derivative of the first, is that practically all the traditional public sector roles are supposed to be played in these countries by the private one. The third invoked problem is the lack of absorption capacity and last but not the least, the problem of fungibility is frequently mentioned. All these arguments however, are tinted with prejudices, being at the same time partial, and non-imaginative. This is because: a) a lack of good governance is a typical trait of early stages of development, and not specific to current LDC; b) although in rich countries for technical reasons some traditional activities of the public sector have recently fallen into the sphere of the private sector, most of these activities cannot be provided by the private sector in LDC without jeopardising sufficient supply; c) non-absorption capacity may perhaps exist in relation with physical investments, but never in relation with human capital (education and health); and d) the problem of fungibility may be corrected when there is only one multilateral institution charged with the distribution of foreign public transfers, according to a mathematical formula in which some activities prone to fungibility could be contemplated as a negative indicator for the provision of funds.

10. We do support a new approach for public international transfers for bridging the economic gap, as an intermediate target to reach global stability. However, the volume of our proposal surpasses by far those of Zedillo and Gordon Brown. These two politicians have recently suggested the convenience of reaching a figure of 0.5%

of donors GDP while we bet on 2%. Neither the Zedillo Report nor suggestions of Gordon Brown or Kofi Anan, have presented the macroeconomic panorama in LDC after finalising the period of implementation. This is a consequence of their focus on non-ambitious targets (such as halving the amount of people under poverty line or reaching a minimum level of literacy for all). In the (unlikely) case that these millennium targets are reached in 2015, this does not guarantee the soothing of hatred and fury among poor and deprived, if the growing gap and exclusion continues. Even worse, since in this case these poor will become better informed, this may encourage a more intense dissatisfaction and retaliatory actions. We are convinced that the 0.5% proposals would lack significant macroeconomic results because their intrinsic insufficiency, and because the distribution of these foreign funds will continue being non-targeted, uncoordinated and fragmented.

11. We do affirm that our proposal for multilateral transfer of funds up to an amount of 2% of the GDP of high-income countries is neither irrational nor exaggerated. Far from that, it is just sufficient to properly reduce the gap in due time and to create a win-win solution for the entire global community. There is no doubt that it will lead to world stability at very low costs for the rich countries in historical terms. We firmly believe that the historical tempo has experienced a dramatic reduction, and the geographical distances have become significantly compressed. Consequently the concept of neighbourhood has also radically changed. Today all of us are neighbours, easily affected by developments in seemingly remote countries. Therefore, in their own interest citizens of rich countries should give the rest the opportunity of living a more decent life. Note that at the end of the day this 2% of GDP of rich countries is much less than the costs of securing the fortress, combined with the economic costs of the regionalisation of trade, and the consequences of the created uncertainty.

12. Concerning the economic implications of our programme, we have to underline that ours is a proposal that goes much further than those of Zedillo, Gordon Brown or Kofi Anan. And not only in terms of annual public transfers, as we have already mentioned, but also in results. Ours, a transfer to lower-middle income LDC of the 2% of the GDP of rich countries, will enable that these LDC grow at an

average of 8%, while their per capita GDP will grow at 6% during the next 24 years. Elemental mathematics indicates that with such a rate it is possible to double the per capita GDP every 12 years. This means that the per capita GDP of these LDC, situated currently at an average of 775 US dollars (in terms of exchange rate), will move (after phasing) to a figure of 1550 US dollars reachable by 2017 and to 3100 dollars by 2029. This forecasted figure, close to the current per capita GDP of Thailand or Costa Rica, means that our strategy for development not only will contribute to alleviate poverty, but also to significantly bridge the economic gap. This is in our view a "necessary condition" for the attainment of global stability (although not a "sufficient condition" for which we propose additional measures).

13. As mentioned before, a UN body provisionally named UNICO should manage the boosted and pooled 2 % budget for development financing. In our view the policy aim of UNICO will be the achievement of an intermediate target, which is fast growth of LDC, necessary for the attainment of the final objective of reaching global peace and human security (international public goods). For operations current UN specialised agencies such as the World Bank, would merge under UNICO, which would only spend its budget in grants (not in loans). This change in approach is a consequence of a far-reaching restatement in the concept of co-operation. The UNICO funds should exclusively be earmarked for financing infrastructure and human capital.

14. The UNICO organisation will count with headquarter and several regional UNICO bodies, called REUNICO in which governments of LDC (after qualifying) will participate. UNICO will allocate funds at national and regional level. The latter will be handled by REUNICO wherein members will approve funds for regional projects up to 20% of total budget for the region. REUNICO members will also monitor the UNICO funded projects in member states. In order to qualify for this, it will be necessary not to be involved in violent interstate or intrastate conflicts condemned by the UN. According to a certain "polynomial formula" to be defined, UNICO will allocate a budget per country and it will establish a general methodology for project appraisal and monitoring.

15.　According to this "polynomial formula", to be defined by UNICO, the funds supplied to countries, should depend, among other variables, on size of population, demographic growth, per capita GDP, degree of indebtedness, public deficit, military expenditure, degree of internal savings, accessibility to international private funds, internal distribution of income, etc. Note that this polynomial formula (somewhat comparable to formulas used in Europe for internal transfers to promote catching up of backward regions) will protect UNICO funding against the fungibility problem. This formula will also enable UNICO to practise a general development policy, favouring certain consented aspects related to the above mentioned variables.

16.　The effects of establishing the UNICO system will be multiple and positive. As a consequence of the huge boosting of development financing, a greater stimulus will finally be introduced in order to modernise the economies of LDC. Note that the so criticised non-accountability of LDC governments, conducive to a theoretical and practical decline of the old ODA, had basically to do with the (irrelevant) amount of the received funds, thus minimising stimuli due to the predictable scant effects on the economy of the recipient country. At the same time, the REUNICO role in monitoring UNICO funded projects in member countries will result in a political stimulus for increasing transparency. Similarly the action of pooling funds by UNICO will enable to overcome the ludicrous previous fragmentation of ODA, which has till date undermined long term planning and accountability at the receiving end. On the other hand, the polynomial formula would allow penalising specific behaviours as for instance keeping high GDP percentage in military expenditure or maintaining population explosion. Finally, the UNICO system will contribute to a larger regional co-operation and it will also encourage conflict resolution.

17.　In relation with current indebtedness of poor countries (Severely Indebted Countries or SIC), the UNICO system will allow to automatically cancel or reschedule the outstanding debts of SIC if they qualify for participation in UNICO. The national budgets of the UNICO system will enable the recipients to choose the timing and the rescheduling period, leaving the concerned SIC a margin for selection of more projects and less debt cancellation or vice versa.

EPILOGUE

The urgency of reassessing the current order.

While finishing this essay, some additional global developments have occurred, such as the provoked and foreseeable failure of Cancun, the failure of the US to gather "third world" support in the case of Iraq, and the incapability of the EU to emerge as a credible player in international issues. These failures are due to the fact that the actions undertaken or the omissions in which the western countries have incurred have been based on non-realistic perceptions of the ongoing political and economic changes, likely conducive in this decade to a structural rupture of the current world order.

Step by step the political and economic gravity centre of the world is visibly shifting to the east. In this altering context Western politicians, mainly worried with the next domestic elections, hardly rise their sight and look into the future, meddling only with short-term internal or external problems (f.i. pension age of their workers, or the exchange rate of the yuan). Notwithstanding that, they should know that some changes in the trend, although hardly perceivable from one year into another, could significantly vary the current correlation of power in the coming 10-15 years.

If we seriously analyse the world today, we have to deduce that some old countries or colonies, such as China and India, that just half a century ago barely counted in the political or economic global game, have today become relevant players, thus politically and commercially attracting neighbouring countries. In addition to the dimension of their economies (respectively the second and the fourth in the ranking of GDP-PPP of nations) and their rapid rates of growth, they have become nuclear powers, maintain huge conventional armies[202], and have enormous and progressively more educated supporting populations. No wonder that in these circumstances their elite's in power have become conscious of the enormous importance of their countries in the current international power-play. A power that according to any logic will tend to grow.

---

202. For updated information on the size (personnel) of the different armies, vide World Bank (2003) "03 World Development Indicators".

Ignoring this new landscape and focussing exclusively on the per capita income gap, the richer Western countries continue enjoying their high per capita consumption levels, while their growth expectations are low against a backdrop of small, stagnant and ageing populations. Forgetting these two crucial unfavourable traits of their economies, they believe that they can continue controlling the international institutions (UN, IMF, World Bank) established after the Second World War, while trusting that their high-tech armies will support their dominance. However, the naked truth is that these evaluations are already partially falsified by reality, while their armies acting unilaterally or in small coalitions lack enough human factor to police the world. Consequently any attempt of indefinitely maintaining the current asymmetric economic and political order is a chimera.

Being rich in per capita terms and in control of the multilateral institutions, while in position to veto any alternative in trade and development policies that allegedly may prejudice them, it seems that they consider themselves as being forever comfortable in a non-accessible citadel. This wrong perception, cyclically belied by history in similar junctures, is producing policies and answers to new facts which, being unfair, cannot be sustainable.

Asymmetries in accessibility in industrial versus agricultural and service markets; defence of a strict one-way direction in the international movements of labour; exigency of strict public and external sector balances to get access to international funds while they themselves (f.i. US, France, Germany) do not eventually comply with these principles; biased, exacted to others but "conveniently implemented by the powerful" treaties of non-proliferation of nuclear weapons; lack of commitment, biased fulfilment or non-implementation of treaties on macro-environment; partial device of sequencing in development policies and trade agendas; and attempts to impose political models to the others, when some of the rich countries behave non democratically in the UN, are simply non-acceptable behaviours in a democratic world.

As history has proven, stubbornly trying to keep unfair positions in the context of a highly informed and economically uneven societies, has no other future than escalation in the form of trade wars, vetoes in multilateral negotiations, formation of regional economic and political blocs, and last but not least continuation of violent actions against the above described unfair framework.

In a world in which the economic power is turning into a more equilibrated one, due to the fast growing of highly populated and industrious Asian countries, which in fact have become leaders of the developing world, it is extremely urgent to reassess the current economic and political order. Only a drastic correction of it, changing it into a more fair and sustainable one, could enable once and for all the construction of a world with the same rules for all players and with similar opportunities for all citizens, as proclaimed in the UN charter.